A BALLET FOR SCOTLAND

A
BALLET
FOR
SCOTLAND

The First Ten Years
of The Scottish Ballet

Noël Goodwin

Canongate Publishing
in association with
Greenleaf Literary Enterprises

First published in 1979
by **Canongate Publishing Ltd**
17 Jeffrey Street,
Edinburgh, Scotland

© **Noël Goodwin 1979**
ISBN (cased) 0 903937 87 5
(paper) 0 903937 88 3

Designed by James Hutcheson. Typesetting by
Whittaker Photoset Ltd., Glasgow. Printed in Great
Britain by The Scolar Press Ilkley

CONTENTS

Dear Peter,
It was you who
made us do the tour.
All my thanks it has
been wonderful love Margot

By Special Arrangement With

Michael Edgley International Pty. Ltd.

Edgley & Dawe Attractions and The Australian Elizabethan Theatre Trust

Proudly Present
The Ballet Event of the Decade

The World's Greatest Ballerina

Dame Margot Fonteyn

Partnered by the Premier Danseur
of the American Ballet Theatre

Ivan Nagy

Together with one of the
United Kingdom's finest ballet companies

The Scottish Ballet

Australian and New Zealand Tour
March-May 1974

Preface

I have danced many times with The Scottish Ballet and have always admired the dedication and enthusiasm of its dancers and management. Now that they are installed in their new premises I know that they will go from strength to strength.

I hope that all who buy this account of their history will enjoy it and will join with me in wishing the Company well.

1.
The Achievement

"Flower Festival at Genzano" with Sally Collard-Gentle and Cristian Addams
(Anthony Crickmay)

In its first ten years the Scottish Ballet has achieved the status of a national company with an international reputation. It has become a source of pleasure and pride to steadily growing audiences, now numbered in the hundreds of thousands every year, while at the same time giving fresh vitality to a theatrical art which has contributed greatly to the heritage of our civilisation. Within Scotland it has put down firm roots in the community it serves, attracted a new respect for the profession it represents, and brought a particular vision of beauty within the reach of all as a desirable element in their quality of life. It is a success story beyond expectation, brought about by dedication, dogged persistence and the devotion of those who have believed in its purpose.

The Scottish Ballet originated at a time when the art of dance was undergoing a widespread transformation in its character and appeal. What has been called the 'dance explosion' is, in the historical sense, one more of the periodic upheavals that affect all the arts in turn. In Britain we have witnessed a surge of interest in dance, especially among younger audiences, which is part of a world-wide trend and which is still continuing. This has helped to consolidate a nationwide basis of seven major UK companies, of which the Scottish Ballet is one,[1] who now receive a share of public funds to perform classical ballet or modern dance on a regular year-round programme. Beyond these is a pro-liferating fringe of about thirty smaller groups, active from time to time, who also receive more limited support to develop additional outlets for dance.

The nature of the Scottish Ballet's purpose is described in the pages that follow, but it needs to be related to this wider context for its achievement to be fully appreciated. The company obviously makes Scotland and Scottish audiences its priority. From time to time, with the support of extra Arts Council funds from London, it gives performances in English centres, usually but not entirely in the north of the country. It has toured abroad: to Australia and New Zealand; to Paris, Madrid, Barcelona, Zurich and other European cities, and during its anniversary year it will revisit Sadler's Wells Theatre in London as well as take part in a new project, the first Inter-national Dance Festival at Bournemouth.

It should be remembered that the Scottish Ballet is seen in London perhaps once in three years, whereas the other major com-panies (except Northern Ballet Theatre) give regular seasons there more frequently. Nevertheless, when the Scottish company last appeared in London, in 1976, there was much admiration for its corporate person-ality and its distinctive identity; for the artistic standards it displayed, and for the range of its repertory from nineteenth-century classics to new works. This could only be brought about by imaginative direction; shrewd and careful administrat-ion, and the enthusiasm that comes from the practical support and encouragement it receives from regular audiences in its home centres.

During its first decade, the Scottish Ballet has expanded from an original twenty dancers with a borrowed orchestra to a com-pany of forty-six dancers on year-round contract; a full-time technical and admin-istration staff of thirty, and an orchestra of 45-55 players (according to the needs of the repertory) who are engaged for the duration of each tour under a permanent music director and orchestra manager. All these involve an annual turnover which has multiplied from just over £100,000 in the first season to about £1,150,000 in 1979-80. Box-office income has risen from nearly £7,000 in the first season to over £300,000 now; annual grants from the Scottish Arts Council have increased from £93,000 to £668,000 in the same period, and local authority support which began at £1,000 in the second year is now at an annual figure of about £50,000.

In this time many dancers have come and gone, but two who were with the company from its inception, Elaine McDonald and Sally Collard-Gentle, have become star dancers in their own right alongside others of the present company such as Patricia Merrin, Andrea Durant and Noriko Ohara. Two other original members, Sue Carlton-Jones and Brian Burn, are now members of

---

[1] The others are the Royal Ballet at Covent Garden; the Sadler's Wells Royal Ballet; Ballet Rambert; London Festival Ballet; London Contemporary Dance Theatre, and Northern Ballet Theatre (Manchester).

Elaine McDonald as Teresina in Act 3 of "Napoli"
(William Cooper)

the teaching staff, while the years between have owed much to the personalities of dancers like Robin Haig, Patricia Rianne, Marian St. Claire, Graham Bart and Kenn Wells. Dancers wholly trained in Scotland through scholarship classes, such as Eleanor Moore, have begun to blossom, and a vocational school for dancers is now in prospect.

A lengthening list of guest dancers testifies to the Scottish Ballet's expanding reputation beyond its own borders, attracting some of the world's super-stars such as Dame Margot Fonteyn, Maina Gielgud, Natalia Makarova, Fernando Bujones, Niels Kehlet, Ivan Nagy and Rudolf Nureyev, as well as the Royal Ballet's David Ashmole, Donald McLeary and Gary Sherwood. The recent history of ballet in Britain suggests that too many guest stars can be frustrating to regular dancers whilst too few can lead to isolation. In the right proportion and the right kind of repertory, however, they can be a valuable and attractive stimulus to the other dancers as well as to the public.

It is unlikely that such visitors would have shown so ready a response without the attraction of repertory as well as the standards of performance. The company has presented an unusually wide spectrum of ballet in ten years, from early nineteenth-century Romantic ballets like La Sylphide and Giselle, through new approaches to two of the Tchaikovsky classics to a range of modern works in classical style. These have included three original full-length ballets (all by Peter Darrell), two of them to specially commissioned scores by British composers, a rare distinction in itself. The extent of the company's achievement in this respect is discussed later on and listed season by season in the Appendix.

The character of the repertory is essentially that of the classical ballet tradition as it has come down to us, in a developing style from one generation to the next. The development of ballet, which emerged in France as a Court entertainment for Louis XIV, was codified into a professional technique in the eighteenth century and blossomed into a

Rudolf Nureyev rehearsing "La Sylphide" with the company in Paris

popular theatrical art in the nineteenth, is told elsewhere in the histories of dance. But it is worth recalling that the seeds of ballet in Britain on a regular professional basis were sown only within our present century, mainly encouraged by the Russian Ballet of Sergei Diaghilev, whose enterprise brought back the classical tradition from Russia to the West.

Diaghilev recruited and trained the three women who between them personified the foundation of a classical tradition in Britain. Dame Marie Rambert began teaching in London in 1920 and in 1926 founded the company which still continues as the Ballet Rambert (although since 1966 it has changed its character to that of a modern dance ensemble). Dame Ninette de Valois became associated with Lilian Baylis at the Old Vic Theatre in London from 1926, and from 1931 at Sadler's Wells Theatre, where the Vic-Wells Ballet formed by her was the basis of the present Royal Ballet. Dame Alicia Markova was the first British prima ballerina, who helped to set the high pro-

fessional standards that both these companies aimed at from the outset; Dame Margot Fonteyn coming into the picture from 1934, when she made her debut at the age of 15.

De Valois operated as far as possible on Diaghilev's principles. She staged the major classics of ballet from the notebooks of the Russian régisseur Nikolay Sergueyev (*Giselle, The Nutcracker* and *Swan Lake* in 1934; *The Sleeping Beauty* in 1939), and supplemented these with the work of emerging choreographers such as Sir Frederick Ashton as well as collaborating with leading composers of the time, who included Vaughan Williams, Sir William Walton and Sir Arthur Bliss. Rambert was more circumscribed by the fact that her company has never acquired a regular base for performance, but she complemented de Valois in constantly acting as a forcing-house for choreographic talent. She first brought Ashton to light, and followed him by encouraging Antony Tudor, Walter Gore, Andrée Howard and Frank Staff in the

The company celebrates the opening of their new premises
(The Scotsman)

1930s, and several more since 1945. Notable among these is Norman Morrice, who was primarily responsible for the change in Ballet Rambert's character in 1966, and who is now Director of the Royal Ballet.

Two more events of the utmost significance for the present flourishing state of classical ballet in the world need to be pinpointed. One was its fate in Soviet Russia after the 1917 revolution when, instead of being swept away as a symbol of imperial decadence (as many activists wanted), it was defended by Anatol Lunasharsky, the first Soviet Commissar of Enlightenment, as a national asset which deserved to be 'made worthy of the proletariat'. In this way was the tradition preserved. The second event was the invitation whereby George Balanchine from the Diaghilev company was enabled to establish the School of American Ballet at New York in 1934, as a base for European classical ballet to parallel the developments of new techniques of modern dance pioneered by Martha Graham, Ruth St. Denis and others.

With the classical tradition kept alive in the USSR, off-shoots of it cultivated in Britain and the USA, the Danish Royal Ballet in Copenhagen as the repository of another branch (the Bournonville repertory), and Paris keeping a few embers feebly flickering, the conditions in the post-war period from 1945 were ripe for classical ballet to become an element of national and civic cultural prestige throughout the world. Whether funded from Government, commercial or private sources, full-time companies devoted to classical dance have become active in almost all European countries, the USSR, much of the Middle East, North and South America, Cuba, China, Japan, Australasia and South Africa. Their success is usually dependent on at least one resident choreographer or director whose works give a company its corporate personality, and on one or more schools of ballet where teachers of distinction can develop a flow of intensively trained young talent year by year.

It was the successful first visit of the then Sadler's Wells Ballet to New York in 1949 which virtually initiated the practice of tours from one country to another on a continuing basis of cultural exchange. The work of this and other British companies was made possible only by the introduction of the principle of public funding through grants from the Arts Council of Great Britain, an independent agency between the Government and the professional artist, set up in the wake of wartime emergency aid given through the Council for the Encouragement of Music and the Arts (CEMA). The Government decided to reopen the Royal Opera House, Covent Garden, as a national headquarters for opera and ballet in 1946, and the Sadler's Wells Ballet was invited to become the resident company there (it received the Royal Charter in 1956). A second company was established in the same year at its old home as the Sadler's Wells Theatre Ballet; among the dancers at its first performance there on 8 April 1946 was one Peter Darrell.

Against this background it will be seen that the Scottish Ballet has virtually compressed into its ten years what it has taken a generation or more for other companies to achieve. Of course, the company started with the advantage of having already been in existence for twelve years at a professional level under a different guise, with a consequent foundation of experience. Also, it began to put down its Scottish roots at the right time, when the public interest in dance was on the increase, and just at a time when it would be helped and encouraged by the new theatres in which its work could be seen, such as the renovated Theatre Royal in Glasgow and the newly-built Eden Court Theatre in Inverness. Not least, it found when it arrived in Scotland that the ground for ballet was not entirely untilled, as the next chapter will show.

2.
The Background

Sylvia Wellman, Victor Maynard rehearsing
Mods & Rockers   (Anthony Crickmay)

When the present Scottish Ballet came about in 1969, it did so in the wake of other pioneering ventures which had already done much for the cause of ballet in Scotland, and some account of them is necessary to the background of the present company. It is a matter of historical record, for instance, that a Scottish National Ballet was formed on a professional basis much earlier, in 1960, and gave its inaugural performance on 23 June that year at the Pitlochry Festival Theatre. The company consisted of fifteen dancers led by Sylvia Macbeth under the artistic direction of Margaret Morris, and it toured to Edinburgh, Glasgow, Aberdeen, Carlisle and Sunderland until, privately financed and without benefit of public subsidy, the losses incurred brought it abruptly to an end a year later.

The technique of Margaret Morris Movement has a history that goes back to the first school she opened in London in 1910, and it continues to be taught under the aegis of an international association which organises an annual summer school such as that at Balls Park, Hertford, in 1978 which was attended by 350 students from many countries. The course involves choreography and improvisation as well as related subjects such as anatomy and physiology. In the early years other Margaret Morris schools were opened in Glasgow, Aberdeen and Manchester, and abroad in Paris and Cannes. After the outbreak of the Second World War in 1939 all these were forced to close with the exception of Glasgow, which became the Celtic Ballet College at 299 West George Street. Here, in 1940, Margaret Morris formed the Celtic Ballet Club of about sixty amateur dancers, who gave about two major productions a year in aid of wartime charities.

From this came a Celtic Ballet company of about fifteen professional dancers which was formed at Glasgow in 1947. It toured at intervals not only to other centres in Scotland but also to France and, in 1954, to the USA for appearances at the famous Jacob's Pillow Dance Festival and in the New England states. The repertory comprised traditional Scottish dances; ballets based on Burns and other subjects (including a *Jungle Drama* by a former Ballets Jooss dancer, Jack Skinner originally trained by Margaret

Morris), and a style based on a form of barefoot modern-dance with Scottish overtones. Margaret Morris Movement sought to combine aesthetic and medical values throughout. 'Other methods may achieve more in either one or the other', she wrote, 'but no other movement synthesises these two seemingly different objectives'.[1]

Margaret Morris long had the ambition of a national ballet company for Scotland. According to Jim Hastie, who was a member of the Celtic Ballet and is now ballet-master for Scottish Opera, she wanted a company that would represent both modern and classical techniques: 'She maintained that you should be able to turn in or turn out at will'. By 1958, she had raised funds to convert part of the Glasgow premises into the Celtic Ballet Theatre, which opened on 5 February 1958 with a programme of her own works. These included the *Skye Boat Song* and *Eastern Celtic Rhythm* (the latter to Rimsky-Korsakov music), as well as a traditional Foursome Reel and an exercise sequence of her own technique.

On this basis she launched an appeal, later the same year, for an endowment fund of £10,000 towards a national company, supported by the then Lord Provost, Myer Galpern, and other civic and educational heads. It was to include an orchestra of 'ten first-class players'. By the following March, a more realistic assessment of costs had raised the target to £50,000 for a company 'at least thirty strong', and after its debut at Pitlochry in the summer of 1960, the Scottish National Ballet launched a six-week tour in April 1961, opening at Her Majesty's Theatre, Carlisle. Songs by Niven Miller and Kay Gordon helped along a varied programme, with dances choreographed by Margaret Morris (*To Catch a Fish; Gods in the Gorbals; The Road to the Isles*), Veronica Bruce (*The White Moth*) and dancer Sylvia Macbeth (*The Harvesters*). Music was confined to two pianos and drums, with the pipes for Highland and other Scottish dances.

Although no public funds were forthcoming, it was reported at the time that the leading New York impresario, Sol Hurok,

---

[1] *Creation and Dance in Life* by Margaret Morris (Peter Owen, 1969, republished 1978).

had 'confirmed' a six-month tour for the company in the USA and Canada, to begin in September 1962, which must have been an encouragement. Press comment on the venture was mixed, however, and somewhat confused whether to relate the programme to what was known of classical ballet or to a superior kind of 'tartan revue'. After the Pitlochry debut *The Scotsman* wrote:[2] 'The appeal of tartan-sashed barefoot girls and kilted boys is not enough to satisfy ballet-lovers: they must see good technique as well', and on the tour a year later, 'The hard work that has been put into the production by Margaret Morris and her company deserves all praise, but the end result will have to be a great deal better if this sort of thing is to go out as representing Scotland'.[3] The venture foundered on the losses incurred, and after the death of her husband Margaret Morris sold her Glasgow premises and returned to London.

Meanwhile, there had been some public comment that the national ballet idea had not involved other dance personalities who might have contributed, such as Marjory Middleton, who opened her Edinburgh

school in 1915, and who directed the Edinburgh Ballet Club founded by Jean Shaw in 1942. 'The object of Marjory Middleton', wrote Peter Noble in a summary of ballet clubs for his 1940s anthology, *British Ballet*,[4] 'is to form the nucleus of a Scottish National Ballet, to be formed in the Autumn of 1949'. Nothing came of this intention, but Marjory Middleton continued to teach classical ballet at a high level, and to serve as a chief examiner in Scotland for the Royal Academy of Dancing until her retirement in 1972. Many of her students went south to continue their training and/or took up professional careers. Among them have been Susan Alexander, Alexander Bennett, Maureen Bruce, John Callander (who became director of the New Zealand Ballet for two years), and Kenneth McCombie, at the time of writing a principal dancer with London Festival Ballet.

For some years the Edinburgh Ballet Club (which still continues on more modest lines) staged an annual production of a major

[2] *The Scotsman*, 24 June 1960.
[3] *The Scotsman*, 2 May 1961.
[4] *British Ballet*, ed Peter Noble (Skelton Robinson).

The Celtic Ballet of Scotland performs Margaret Morris's "Skye Boat Song" during their visit to Jacob's Pillow (Jack Mitchell)

classic ballet each Autumn, its ensemble of students supplemented by professionals such as Mona Inglesby and Oleg Briansky, who led *Swan Lake* in the 1960s, and Robin Haig, a later member of the Scottish Theatre Ballet, in *Giselle* with Alexander Bennett (who was to become ballet-master of Western Theatre Ballet). The regular conductor was the journalist and broadcaster Neville Garden. Some original ballets were also staged, including *Pavane*, the first two-act ballet on the subject of Mary, Queen of Scots, with choreography by Marjory Middleton and music by Leighton Lucas.

Concurrently with this activity Veronica Bruce, already mentioned in connection with the Celtic Ballet, formed her own Cygnet Ballet just after the war which received some of the first public subsidy given to ballet in Scotland by CEMA (the Council for the Encouragement of Music and the Arts), forerunner of the Arts Council of Great Britain, and later from the Scottish Arts Council. Veronica Bruce studied with Tamara Karsavina, Lubov Egorova, Anton Dolin and Cleo Nordi, who became artistic adviser and created some ballets for the Cygnet company, which comprised a nucleus of 12—15 dancers. Karsavina and Idzikowsky helped to stage productions of such works as *Swan Lake* Act 2 and *Le Spectre de la Rose*, and Nordi mounted *Chopiniana*; the company also appeared with the Glyndebourne Opera at the early Edinburgh Festivals from 1947. It continued into the 1950s, and was probably the first classical ballet company to tour the Hebrides, Orkney and Shetland.

Some years later Veronica Bruce returned to her family estate at Dunphail in Moray where, in addition to opening a school in Forres, she converted a squash court into a small theatre, which she called the Intimate Ballet Theatre. It seated about seventy and had a stage twenty-four feet square, and in 1961 the first of several summer festivals was organised with the help of Robin Anderson (the present Administrator of the Scottish Ballet) who built a lighting-board, scenery and acted as all-purpose stage manager for several years. During two weeks each summer, performances of classical ballet were given with students from the Cygnet Ballet School in Forres and

Rehearsals at Veronica Bruce's Intimate Ballet Theatre near Forres in the 60s.

professional principals, and these festivals continued to 1975.

Among the fellow-teachers who sent talented pupils to these festivals was Catherine Marks, who formed the Glasgow Theatre Ballet in the early 1960s with both professional and amateur dancers from the school she opened in Glasgow soon after the war. She was classically trained as a student of Audrey de Vos and she worked with Lydia Kyasht, whose Ballets de la Jeunesse Anglaise was active in London during the war years. For several years the Glasgow Theatre Ballet made short tours up and down Scotland for three to four weeks twice a year, also with Robin Anderson as stage manager. Catherine Marks choreographed some original ballets including *Derby Day*; Walter Gore staged *Comin' through the Rye*, and in 1968 there was a production by Alexander Bennett of *La Sylphide* using the original Schneitzhoeffer music; Bennett danced James, with Noreen Sopwith as the Sylphide and Jim Hastie as Gurn. A present member of the Scottish Ballet, Paulene Laverty, is a former student of the Glasgow Theatre School of Ballet, which still continues.

The formation of a permanent ballet company for Scotland was an idea often cherished, sometimes declared and always present for many years, but while none of the organisations mentioned had the scope or the resources to establish it alone, neither did they seek the kind of purposeful collaboration which might have attracted public subsidy and so made it a reality. Instead they saw most of their most talented pupils from Scotland go south to make their careers, and when the time did come that circumstances made it right for Scotland to have a resident ballet company, it was from the south that an already established company was found to be available.

Like so much else on the dance scene in Britain, Western Theatre Ballet came about through one woman's vision. Elizabeth West, who was killed by an avalanche at the age of thirty-five in 1962, while on holiday in the Swiss Alps, trained as a dancer with Edouard Espinosa and Muriel Carpenter, and turned to drama at the Bristol Old Vic Theatre School, starting work at the Bristol

Old Vic in 1946. As well as acting and dancing, she became a theatre choreographer both there and for the Shakespeare Festival at Stratford-upon-Avon, and in 1954 she reached London's West End in Julian Slade's musical, *The Duenna*, where one of her fellow-dancers was a certain Peter Darrell, formerly of the Royal Ballet School and the Sadler's Wells Theatre Ballet.

At Elizabeth West's invitation Darrell went to Bristol and choreographed *Celeste and Celestina* for the Bristol School of Dancing, followed by an experimental work on a topical subject (the atom bomb) which later became *Impasse*. After starting a small group independently, the West of England Ballet, Elizabeth West gathered a dozen dancers together to form Western Theatre Ballet, with Darrell as co-director and dancer, and the prospect of one month's tour. From the outset she wanted to make it a regional company, based on Bristol because that was where she worked, but with the ultimate objective of a complete lyric theatre for the city, including an opera house. She also wanted to take ballet to places, notably in the south-west of England, where live performances were seldom if ever seen.

But it was to be ballet with a difference. As Peter Darrell has said: 'We wanted to kill the image of an insular little group of pretty, tarlataned sylphs. Liz wanted to bring the acting and dramatic side out far stronger. Right from the word go, we wanted to emphasise acting and acting-training as much as dance and dance-training'.[5] Western Theatre Ballet accordingly made its debut in Devonshire, at Dartington Hall, on 24 June 1957, with a repertory of six ballets, an Arts Council grant of £500, and a company who included Brenda Last, Hazel Merry, Suzanne Musitz, Erling Sunde and Oliver Symons. They made a short tour of the West country, gave a week at the Bristol Theatre Royal and wound up with a week at the tiny Arts Theatre in London, where a review by Clive Barnes made the prophetic comment: 'Here is a small beginning that could develop into something really important'.[6]

---

5 'Peter Darrell talks to *Dance and Dancers*', June 1963
6 *Dance and Dancers*, October 1957.

Robin Haig in "Home"   (Anthony Crickmay)

Writing years later, the editor of *Dance and Dancers*, Peter Williams, recalled of the company's inaugural performance: 'Undoubtedly the most important work that night was Peter Darrell's *The Prisoners*, to Bartók music and designed by Barry Kay. Not only was this a fine work but it started an association of Darrell with Liz West that was to build up a repertory of dance works using contemporary themes. Today, when most companies have works of this kind, it might be forgotten that in 1957 this was something unique in British ballet . . . Western Theatre Ballet not only pioneered dance-drama but built up the foundations of regional ballet, although many years were to pass before this was to be generally considered an essential part of the pattern in this country's artistic policy'.[7]

Those many years began with a hand-to-mouth existence on minimal Arts Council support for occasional tours, and whatever other work could be obtained at the Bristol Old Vic or in pantomime, while the founder-director went around trying to raise money. One report gives a graphic illustration of her efforts: 'Miss West, with the simplicity and tenacity of a St Francis, trusted in providence, and whenever a benefactor failed to turn up, she organised eccentric fund-raising schemes of her own. Once she asked Bristol citizens to ring College Green with half-crowns. Costumed, the company would ''sell'' steps to passers-by — for 2s 6d, a grand jeté; for 10s, a pas de deux. It was a brilliant premise for musical comedy, and comedy ensued: on the appointed day there was a clap of thunder, the heavens opened and a bedraggled company in soggy point shoes and wilting tutus hurled themselves about the Green before a sparse and astonished audience of mackintoshed shoppers. They realised £50[8]

More substantial sums were provided by benevolent shareholders and directors under the chairmanship of Mrs. T.F. Hewer, and a few donations, while the indefatigable founder went abroad and found tour dates in 1959 in Rome, followed by Ostend and Knokke. In Belgium they were seen by

[7] 'The 21 Years that Changed British Ballet', *Dance and Dancers*, January 1971.

[8] Charles Bricker in *The Illustrated London News*, 9 April 1966.

Western Theatre Ballet in "Street Games"
(Anthony Crickmay)

Maurice Huisman, administrator of the Théâtre Royale de la Monnaie at Brussels, who brought a turning-point in WTB fortunes by engaging the company there for three months. They not only performed their own repertory in Brussels, but also combined with Maurice Béjart and Janine Charrat, and they appeared the next year in a joint season at Sadler's Wells Theatre, notably in Béjart's production of *The Rite of Spring*. Their Arts Council grant was raised to £3,000, and the Calouste Gulbenkian Foundation awarded them £7,500 spread over three years. A Spanish tour, however, brought a loss of £2,000 with the company stranded and their equipment impounded: a crisis from which they were rescued by an anonymous donor.

At the end of 1960 WTB made its first acquaintance with Scotland in a Glasgow Christmas show, *A Wish for Jamie*, followed by a tour, then returned north again in 1961 for its debut at the Edinburgh Festival, when Cleo Laine and the Royal Ballet's Anya Linden were guest stars in Kenneth MacMillan's first version of Brecht and Weill's *The Seven Deadly Sins*. This formed part of a triple bill with *Salade* (Darrell/Milhaud) and *Renard* (Alfred Rodrigues/Stravinsky). A newcomer to the company at this time was Muriel Large, who joined as administrator on a three-weeks engagement, and stayed for nearly twelve years. There was another Christmas season at Glasgow — in Robert Helpmann's production of *Aladdin* — and the city also later saw the premiere of a significant Darrell ballet, *Jeux*, to Debussy music, at the Citizens' Theatre in 1963.

Meanwhile, Darrell had become sole artistic director of the company after Elizabeth West's tragic death, and he took them on the company's first visit to the USA in 1963. They appeared for two weeks at the Jacob's Pillow Festival, and on a short tour which brought them to New York as part of the Rebecca Harkness Kean Summer Festival at the Delacourt Theatre in Central Park. A succession of ballets that finally established the character of the company continued with Darrell's daring *Mods and Rockers '63* (to songs by the Beatles);

Peter Darrell and the original dancers of Western
Theatre Ballet

Donna Day Washington in "Breakaway"

Houseparty (1964; commissioned by BBC television, with a scenario by John Hopkins); *Lysistrata* (1964; an updating of the classic legend in a scenario by Benny Green, with music by John Dankworth); *Home* (1965; on a subject of mental derangement, with the Royal Ballet's Nadia Nerina as a guest) and *Sun into Darkness* (1966; on a scenario by David Rudkin) and the first three-act ballet with an original score (by Malcolm Williamson, now Master of the Queen's Music) since *The Prince of the Pagodas* (John Cranko/Benjamin Britten) at Covent Garden in 1957.

WTB encouraged other choreographic talent, notably from the Canadian-born dancer Laverne Meyer, who became Darrell's associate director and subsequently established the Northern Dance Theatre in Manchester. He made a distinctive contribution with the first ballets in Britain to music by Webern (*The Web*, 1962) and Berg (*Reconciliations*, 1963, and *Trial*, 1966). The company also gave the British premieres of such other works as MacMillan's *Las Hermanas* in 1966, and Flemming Flindt's *The Lesson* the following year, as well as the premieres of works by Jack Carter, Ray Powell, Peter Wright and others. During this time Peter Cazalet emerged as a major new talent in ballet design, and from 1965 the company was given an association with the Sadler's Wells Opera (now the English National Opera) in the artistic direction of the opera ballets, both in London and on tour.

When WTB celebrated its tenth anniversary at Sadler's Wells Theatre in 1967, the eighteen dancers included six who were later to make the transfer to Scotland: Bronwen Curry and Elaine McDonald; Brian Burn, Peter Cazalet, Sean Cunningham and Ashley Killar. Western Theatre Ballet gave its final performance under that name not quite in the city where it all began, but in nearby Bath, at the Theatre Royal on 15 March 1969. At the end of Walter Gore's *Street Games*, long a favourite in the repertory, Robert Verbrugge had the role of chalking up on a wall the usual *graffito* 'Mary loves Bill'. For the once and only time, he managed to incorporate rather more strokes of the chalk into the steps and eventually produced the inscription, 'Peter loves Muriel' instead.

'So that was WTB', wrote John Percival in his review of the last performance,[9] and he went on to add: 'Scottish Theatre Ballet will be different, but it will inherit some good traditions: a sense of drama, for one, and a sense of humour, for another. Also, and this is the most valuable, a belief that ballet ought to make sense. There were some rough moments in WTB's twelve years, but altogether they were twelve enjoyable years. If STB is as much fun to watch, lucky Scotland'.

[9] *Dance and Dancers*, May 1969.

3.
The Beginnings

"Ephemeron" with Elaine McDonald and Peter Cazalet (Anthony Crickmay)

The first formal announcement that Western Theatre Ballet would move to Glasgow and become Scottish Theatre Ballet was made early in August 1968. It was a joint statement by the chairmen of two companies, Mrs. T.F. Hewer for Western Theatre Ballet and Robin Orr for Scottish Opera, thereby indicating that the basis of activity was originally planned as some form of association between them. In the words of the statement: 'While the tradition of both companies will be preserved, each will be able to benefit from the artistic resources of the other'. It was expected that the plan would operate from the Autumn of 1969, and that the ballet company would share the facilities of the then recently-opened Scottish Opera Centre. The details were to be worked out at further meetings with the Scottish Arts Council.

Reporting this at the time,[1] Conrad Wilson, music critic for *The Scotsman,* wrote: 'The link between the two companies promises to be a very exciting one for the future development of musical theatre in Scotland, and will serve to create the kind of set-up that already exists in many Continental houses, where opera and ballet productions are staged by sister companies under one roof'. He added: 'It will certainly provide one more reason for both Edinburgh and Glasgow to get on with the building of first-class modern theatres as soon as possible. In addition, the presence of a company such as Western Theatre Ballet in Scotland should be an enormous stimulus to our audiences, to Scottish Opera . . . and to our already-existent part-time ballet groups'.

There were some mixed feelings on the part of those groups that one or other of them, or some form of amalgamation, had not been made the basis of a full-time Scottish company. However, it was emphasised that the Scottish Arts Council wanted to establish a company at the highest professional standard and, the situation in Scotland being what it was, the best of Scottish talent found that professional careers could only be furthered in the south. With a company of WTB's reputation available and prepared to make the change, it seemed less risky, artistically and financially, to bring in an existing professional company than to attempt to build one only from what remained of local resources.

Meetings were accordingly arranged between the WTB management and the leading personalities in Scottish ballet, and the hope was expressed that the company would find some way to use the best of Scottish talent when possible. One plan mooted at the time was to have a large-scale classical ballet company with a corps de ballet who could include local dancers, but Peter Darrell and his board of directors were adamant that the transplant would only flourish and bear fruit if it took root on the basis of the company's existing character. New versions of suitable classical ballets might be added later, when the company was ready for them.

Darrell understood from the outset that to succeed the company had somehow to become a national company for Scotland. To do this he would need to go cautiously at first to seek out, as he put it, 'the temperature of the country'. He believed that the company and its repertory should be so grafted on to the existing arts and entertainment scene in Scotland that it would become indigenous in its character, and would grow out of the country and the interests of its potential audiences, not seem to be imposed on them. To do this involved as much touring as possible outside the main centres, and WTB was in any case a company experienced in that. To any doubts that they might not spend enough time in their new milieu, Darrell replied categorically: 'Our first duty is to Scotland; England is for touring'.

Towards implementing this general policy Darrell and Muriel Large were in Glasgow in January 1969 to audition pupils from Scottish dancing schools as possible recruits for the company. The fact that they found none of sufficient standard gave rise before long to comments that Scottish Theatre Ballet was a company of 'foreigners'.[2] Nevertheless, with the support of his board, Darrell was unprepared to compromise professional standards for the sake of local

---

[1] *The Scotsman,* 7 August 1968.

[2] Ten years later, the *Glasgow Herald* happily published a picture of Scottish Ballet dancers from six countries under the caption 'Scottish Ballet's international face' (6 December 1978).

pride or whatever, but he recognised already that means would have to be found for training new dancers in Scotland and, before even the first year's activity was over, plans were made to bring this about.

Meanwhile, by the end of 1968, the discussions had crystallised for the immediate future. It was confirmed that the company would be known as Scottish Theatre Ballet and be based in Glasgow from the Spring in an association with Scottish Opera, with whom it would collaborate in a major production of the Berlioz epic, *The Trojans*, at Glasgow and Edinburgh in May. There was an assurance from the Scottish Arts Council of special funds for a separate orchestra for the ballet company in its independent programmes, and an agreement that STB should give one London season a year in addition to its Scottish commitments. It was also intended that STB would become responsible for 'finding and training dancers' for any ballets required in Scottish Opera's own productions.

Constant reports of a merger led to fears in some quarters that the ballet company might be absorbed by Scottish Opera and become only an adjunct to it. This was put to Mrs. Hewer, who continued as chairman of the STB board of directors. She replied that the Scottish Arts Council had 'completely accepted' the principle of the ballet company's independence: 'We will keep our separate identity. There is no question of us being swallowed up', she maintained.[3] Indeed, it was hoped that the opera and ballet companies would begin to plan a joint repertory, some of which would involve an active collaboration, and these works would be 'chosen by both companies'. In the event, it was soon found that the development of a ballet repertory would need to be governed by a quite different policy from that of the opera.

At first, however, the ballet and opera companies were more or less equal partners in a double-bill which opened at the Perth Theatre on 9 April 1969. It consisted of Robin Orr's one-act opera, *Full Circle*, which Scottish Opera had premiered the

---

[3] *Bristol Evening Post*, 24 January 1969.

The company in the original production of "La Ventana"   (Anthony Crickmay)

previous year, followed by the ballet company in Bournonville's 1854 classic, *La Ventana*, which Hans Brenaa of the Royal Danish Ballet had staged for WTB, also in the previous year. Elaine McDonald and Peter Cazalet took the principal roles with deft assurance of style, and the celebrated pas de trois was admirably danced by Susan Carlton, Donna Day Washington and Kenn Wells. The choice of a Danish classic to inaugurate the company presaged a continuing association with the Danish repertory which later brought successful productions of the two-act *La Sylphide* and the three-act *Napoli*.

Less than a month later, on 3 May 1969, Scottish Theatre Ballet appeared for the first time at the King's Theatre, Glasgow,[4] in a direct collaboration with Scottish Opera for the memorable production of *The Trojans*. This made musical history by being the first time anywhere that both parts of the opera (*The Capture of Troy* and *The Trojans at Carthage*) had been performed *uncut* in a single evening. The memory of Janet Baker's tragically eloquent Dido and of

Alexander Gibson's vivid conducting of Berlioz is still with this writer — they set a standard for the opera which later productions at Covent Garden have certainly not surpassed. And there were the dancers of Scottish Theatre Ballet, involved right from the opening scene, and led by Elaine McDonald in the poignant silent mime role of the widowed Andromache in Part 1.

---

4 In the printed programme for this season, the first list of STB personnel comprised Peter Darrell (Artistic Director), Colin Graham (Artistic Advisor), Kenneth Alwyn (Musical Director), and the following dancers:

Susan Carlton	Brian Burn
Bronwen Curry	Peter Cazalet
Sally Collard-Gentle	Pedro del Busto
Caroline Douglas	Sean Cunningham
Elaine McDonald	Terence James
Patricia Rianne	Ashley Killar
Jenny Staples	Gernot Petzold
Juliet Tooby	Domy Reiter
Vreny Verina	Tatsuo Sakai
Donna Day Washington	Kenn Wells

Staff: Muriel Large (Administrator); Harry Haythorne (Assistant to Artistic Director); Ian McGinnes (Stage Manager); Lesley Bull (Wardrobe mistress).
Board of Directors: Mrs. T. F. Hewer (Chairman); Richard Hawkins, Russell Brown, Lord Chewton, E. Kelland-Espinosa, William Glock, Miss Mary Hoskyn, Mrs. Charity James, Owen Reed, John Steer, Mrs G. R. Strauss.

Dame Janet Baker and the company in "The Trojans"

"Paquita" with Elaine McDonald and Graham Bart   (Anthony Crickmay)

Some time before, it had been announced that Darrell was engaged on a new full-length ballet for the company, and to allow him to concentrate on this the choreography for *The Trojans* was undertaken by his former WTB associate, Laverne Meyer. Meyer had by then put into effect at Manchester the plans that were to bring about the birth of Northern Dance Theatre (since 1977, Northern Ballet Theatre) in the following Autumn. For *The Trojans* he created sequences of celebratory dances, stylised 'public games', and classical divertissements, including nymphs on point for the 'Royal Hunt and Storm'. All these enriched the opera's visual presentation although, as I wrote then, it must be heartbreaking for any choreographer to know that the moment his responsibility finishes, Dido is going to sing, rather pointedly, "I am weary of all this dancing" before launching into the sublime love-duet with Aeneas.

Two nights after this, on 5 May, STB appeared in its own right with *La Ventana*, again in a programme begun by the opera company in *Full Circle*, but enlarged to a triple bill with a new ballet as the centrepiece — Gillian Lynne's *Breakaway*. This was something more in keeping with the WTB tradition of ballets on contemporary social themes, and word had already circulated of its nature and content. As one newspaper report put it: 'Love-making and partner-swapping will be shown on a Scottish stage next month — in a ballet. Dancers dressed in black and flesh-coloured tights will simulate the sex act in a 35-minute ballet entitled "Breakaway" '. Was there a note of regret in the further line: 'But no one will take their clothes off on stage'[5]?

In fact Gillian Lynne, who had worked extensively in different kinds of theatre (including operas, musicals, *The Owl and the Pussycat* for WTB and the dances in the film version of *Half a Sixpence*), had contrived an illustration of youthful mores with a jazzy score by Barry Booth. It was best summarised in Richard Buckle's review: 'A series of easy whimsical dances which present a slight story of teenagers of today aghast at the idea of two of their tribe falling seriously in love. Peter Cazalet, the company's versatile leading man, paired off with delightful Elaine McDonald, leaving the others, led by a comparative newcomer, Kenn Wells, aghast'.[6]

More fundamentally, Scottish Theatre Ballet had made the point that its artistic policy for the future would combine respect for the classical tradition on the one hand, with awareness of new dramatic themes capable of being illuminated by dance, exactly as WTB had done in the previous decade. The programme with *La Ventana* and *Breakaway* was initially given two performances in Glasgow and one in Edinburgh. The Scottish music critics, coping bravely with an unfamiliar idiom, were enthusiastic; the public seemed to like what they saw; there were no charges of subverting Scottish morals, and Darrell and his colleagues could go ahead with plans to consolidate the company's first impact.

---

[5] *Scottish Daily Mail*, 24 April 1969.

[6] *Sunday Times*, 11 May 1969.

4.
Peter Darrell

When Peter Darrell arrived in Scotland with the company he had assembled for the first season of the Scottish Theatre Ballet, he was not only a director of experience in his work with the WTB, but also a choreographer who had ranged more widely than his ballets for that company. He had created other works in Canada, Denmark, Germany, Holland and Switzerland; had acquired valuable experience in television as well as in the theatre; had been involved in musicals in London and Paris, and had danced with several companies since his debut in April 1946 as one of the original members of Sadler's Wells Theatre Ballet — the new company established there after the Sadler's Wells Ballet had become resident at the Royal Opera House, Covent Garden. Among his fellow-dancers in the new company was another director-to-be in Kenneth MacMillan, and both were straight from the Sadler's Wells Ballet School (now the Royal Ballet School).

Darrell was born at Richmond, Surrey, on 16 September 1929, and while he was at ballet school he realised that his inclination already was much more for choreography than for dancing. He spent much of his time working out bits and pieces in the classroom, feeling the need to express his own ideas more than those of others. He responded keenly to the dramatic theatre — to plays and films, being consciously influenced by many of these, in particular the 'new wave' of French films in the 1950s. Their freedom of movement related to thought and feeling — a sense of 'inconsequential inevitability' as he once called it — made a lasting impression. He believed that a similar approach could invigorate the medium of dance, and he longed to be able to show in choreography as much as playwrights can communicate in words.

With Western Theatre Ballet, as we have seen, he was able to develop these ideas, and to relate dance more closely to dramatic theatre. Until recently he was the only British choreographer to invite collaborations from outside authors and playwrights in preparing balletic scenarios, as John Mortimer did for Home (1965), and David Rudkin for Sun into Darkness (1966). The figure of the outsider — the human being, male or female, in a situation of stress that is potentially explosive — is still a subject that engages his imagination. It recurs frequently in his own ballets up to the present time — most recently the Woman in Five Rückert Songs (1978) — but he no longer feels it so necessary to be as realistic in detail as in the 1960s. Now it is the essence that he will tend to abstract and put into dance form.

Darrell has always taken a somewhat wary view of life, believing that nothing is quite what it seems, and that everybody has more to them than might at first appear. Life being usually no bed of roses in any sense, it is the way people react to an inevitable situation that interests his creative imagination. If they explode, so much the better. He has always had an ambition to direct in the theatre (he engaged Colin Graham, a distinguished theatre and opera director, as artistic advisor when he was with WTB). When he begins a new ballet, he will explain the overall idea to the dancers first, and then, like Ashton, create on them in detail on the rehearsal floor. Working with alternative casts, so essential in a repertory and touring company, he is not above changing some quite important element to suit individual dancers — even to having two different endings if that would show both to better advantage.

Now that he can see more clearly the path for the Scottish Ballet, and now that the temperature has changed in response to the company's achievement, he is concerned that what is new and original should grow out of the needs of the artistic repertory, not be sought for its own sake. He once defined originality as 'just an aspect of artistic honesty', adding: 'Just as playwrights don't feel compelled to coin new words, so a choreographer can express himself through a comparatively conventional classical vocabulary. But the use must be honest, apposite and, if you like, arresting. Ashton and Balanchine invent comparatively little, but their choreographic thought is consistently inventive. This is what matters'. Asked what he understood by inventiveness, he replied: 'A fresh approach in knitting steps together, and a new light on the music and the way it is used'.[1]

This is the principle that has underlain all

[1] 'Peter Darrell talks to Dance and Dancers', June 1963.

his work as a choreographer and director, whether in his own ballets or in his new approaches to established classics. As a director he maintains that it is the needs of the repertory which must come first, and his own creative ideas or desires are governed by that. This is a basic policy related to the company's status as the national ballet for Scotland, and to the interests of its audiences. As far as it is possible to see, Darrell believes that a similar balance of repertory will continue, and he is adamant that he wants to involve more living composers and to work with them in a creative way for the art of dance: 'If that blood stops coming', he told the present writer, 'we're dead'.

It is partly this thoughtful balance between the new and the classical that has so quickly given the company an international as well as a national reputation, and ensured a high level of individual dancers in its ranks. They are also attracted by the friendly informality of a directorial approach which is strong and authoritative without being autocratic. The late John Cranko transformed by similar methods the once-provincial Stuttgart Ballet into a company of international acclaim, and Darrell's achievement is comparable. In return for his confidence in the dancers' ability, as well as his insistence on stretching the limits of their capabilities, they have more than once given him a loyalty beyond not only the call of duty but also beyond the feelings of admiration and affection that have knit the company together.

His personality can be reticent, to the extent of refusing to take curtain-calls even after an important premiere of his own work, but it expands when he is among friends he has come to know well. Combined with his professionalism, this has brought a ready acceptance of invitations on the part of a distinguished list of guest dancers, from Dame Margot Fonteyn onwards, who have expressed pride as well as pleasure at having roles created by him, or at appearing in existing works with the company. It also means that the Scottish Ballet can attract resident dancers of the right calibre who are anxious to work with him. Today there is a

Peter Darrell rehearsing Elaine McDonald
(William Cooper)

steady stream of applicants, by letter and by telephone, from as far abroad as Australia and the USA as well as at home.

In recruiting new talent fresh from graduation, it is not always the prize student who engages his attention. It might even be an apparently quite unprepossessing dancer he chooses — because he has found a quality of individuality which he can encourage and develop, then use to advantage. Beyond the technical expertise, which is obviously essential, he looks first for musicality in the dancer's movement and phrasing; then for an awareness of the outside world beyond the dancer's professional interests and, with this, an open-minded response to ideas as well as clarity of thought about them. With a company repertory related to creative interpretation, not to mere repetition, Darrell has no use for a dancer who is blinkered in outlook, whether on matters of general or professional interest.

He recognises that the Scottish Ballet of today cannot grow much larger in numbers, nor has he any wish for it to do so. As the company approaches its tenth anniversary in Scotland, his immediate concern is to consolidate its technique as an ensemble; to look constantly for improved methods and styles of presentation, and to encourage as much if not more adventurousness in the repertory for the future. He takes nothing for granted, but he has a justifiable pride in having brought about the visionary hopes of Elizabeth West over twenty years ago in proving that a ballet company does not have to be anchored in London to succeed. Now he is concerned that Scotland should have the kind of range and variety of ballet which can be enjoyed in London or New York.

"Such Sweet Thunder"   (William Cooper)

34

5.
Putting Down Roots

"Beauty and the Beast"   (Anthony Crickmay)

For the first four seasons from the Autumn of 1969 to the Spring of 1973, the Scottish Theatre Ballet steadily put down wider and stronger roots in the community by developing the scope of its activities: in repertory, in touring, in experimental work, in training and in education. An initial grant from the Scottish Arts Council for 1969-70 was £93,000, and the company went ahead with performances of works earlier produced by Western Theatre Ballet, to which new ballets were soon added. A week at Perth at the end of October 1969 brought revivals of Flemming Flindt's *The Lesson* (1963) and Clover Roope's *Spectrum* (1967), and an earnest of Peter Darrell's intentions in the matter of other choreographers was his engagement of John Neumeier to create *Frontier*. Neumeier, a former member of the Stuttgart Ballet, was then about to embark on his first directorship (at Frankfurt), and is now one of Europe's leading choreographers.

Immediately after this the company went south to give the premiere, on 19 November, of Darrell's *Beauty and the Beast*, its first full-evening production, which had long been arranged for Sadler's Wells Theatre. The two-act ballet had an original score composed for it by the Edinburgh-born Thea Musgrave, as well as a novel approach on Darrell's part to the nature of the fable, and its character is discussed further in Chapter 8. The first reactions were moderately warm, the metropolitan Press being divided mainly between those who welcomed new directions for dance and others who fancied themselves guardians of the 'classical tradition'. It is of interest to note, however, that the ballet won a more popular success with Press and public alike when the company returned north and staged it at Edinburgh in December.

At this point the history of the Scottish Theatre Ballet nearly came to an abrupt and untimely end through a dispute over policy and management. Earlier in the year Darrell had asked if a full-time associate could be engaged to assist him. In December the management board announced the appointment of David Reynolds as overall Director of the Scottish Theatre Ballet. Reynolds, a former dancer, was then assistant music director at the Arts Council of Great Britain. It became clear that his appointment was to be superior to Darrell as artistic director, and that his policy for the company's future, mainly fragmented into small touring groups with a basically educational purpose and only seldom performing as a whole, was alien to Darrell's own intentions.

Darrell consequently announced his resignation, as did Muriel Large as administrator. They were followed by all the dancers and the production staff, whose contracts were due to end the next March, and who confirmed their decision after talking it over with the new appointee. For almost two months it looked as if the Scottish Theatre Ballet was about to become a board without a company, and Spring performances due to be given in conjunction with the Scottish Opera season were cancelled. A compromise was eventually reached at the end of January whereby Darrell and Reynolds were to become co-directors with separate responsibilities: Darrell for the artistic character of the company as a whole, and Reynolds for educational work and 'forward planning'. The latter project did not progress very far, however, and Reynolds left at the end of his first year's contract.

The uncertainty over the company's future reduced its performances in the early part of 1970, but it became a year for exploration in several directions. Experimental work was quickly encouraged, with a workshop programme of six ballets at Glasgow's Close Theatre Club in January which led to some television interest: an excerpt from one of the works, Ashley Killar's *Match for Three Players*, was shown on BBC-tv in Scotland. Darrell wanted the ballet for the regular repertory, but difficulties over the music copyright prevented it. The workshop venture as a whole, however, led to another experimental programme some months later under the title of *Ploys*, which was first staged in London during September at The Place.[1] Again six works were performed,

---

[1] The Place, Duke's Road, London, WC1, is the headquarters of the Contemporary Dance Trust, which controls the London Contemporary Dance Theatre (directed by Robert Cohan) and the London School of Contemporary Dance.

including a repeat of Killar's and one, *Sleepers*, by Stuart Hopps, who was to become the company's associate director a year later.

The declared intention of *Ploys* was to explore 'kinetic possibilities outside the range of the proscenium stage', and although the works attracted some adverse as well as sympathetic reviews, the programme was judged to be sufficiently promising to be repeated in Edinburgh, Glasgow and at the Newcastle Festival. Indeed, the Chairman of the board, Mrs. Hewer, wrote in her Annual Report for 1970-71: 'It is planned that workshop opportunities shall be available annually for members of the company, and that experimental programmes, which are of particular interest to young audiences, shall be given from time to time'. Such a policy has since been followed more consistently and enterprisingly than by most other companies in Britain.

Adequate rehearsal space, always a fundamental problem, was brought about by converting, with the aid of funds from the Scottish Arts Council, a floor of the Scottish Opera centre at Elmbank Crescent, Glasgow, into two studios and wardrobe space, which were ready in May 1970. Unfortunately there was no room for the offices as well, which remained at Woodside Terrace, and all the company's activities did not come together under one roof until the present headquarters in West Princes Street was first occupied in 1978. At Elmbank Crescent two new works were prepared for a London season in July: Clover Roope's *Points of Contact*, and Darrell's highly unconventional *Herodias*, with its a-sexual Salome portrayed by Kenn Wells. 'Does this company want to dance or act or what?' was one irritated newspaper comment, to which the answer might well have been given: 'Yes!'

An important step for the future was the start of free Saturday classes, from September, for talented students within reach of Glasgow. Schools and teachers were invited to send pupils for audition and more than ninety came forward, all girls, of whom eleven were chosen initially and three more were soon added. Those selected took

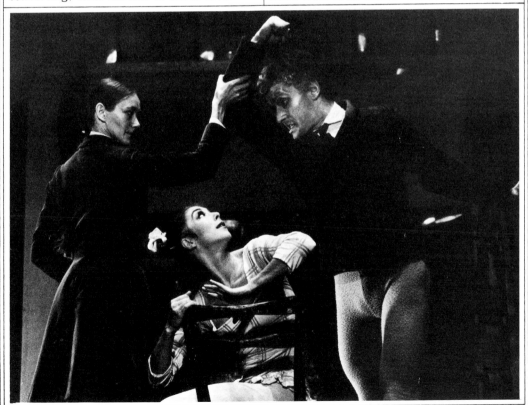

"The Lesson" with Elaine McDonald, Andrea Durant and Graham Bart   (Anthony Crickmay)

company class with Harry Haythorne or Gordon Aitken (who had been formally appointed ballet-master), and they were still required to take at least one other class a week with their own teachers, so that there should be no question of 'poaching'. The hope for this 'preliminary step', as the Chairman's Report for the year put it, was that it 'will lead to the establishment in Scotland of a school which will enrich the educational facilities for dance, and give to young dancers north of the border a training which would prepare them for entry to any major company'.

That school has yet to come about, but it remains a major objective of present policy. With the support of dance teachers in nominating pupils, whose numbers doubled to more than thirty within two years and included some boys, the Saturday classes soon proved their worth. Students, who had to be at least fourteen years old and ranged up to nineteen, benefited from the experience of working with professional dancers, and some were occasionally given stage experience as 'extras' in major productions. Darrell's hope that the sources of untapped talent in Scotland would eventually yield

some fully professional dancers for the company was fulfilled when Eleanor Moore became the first Saturday student to graduate into the company in April 1972.

The distinction of being the first Scottish-born dancer on regular contract, however, belongs to Keri Stewart, who joined the company in March 1971. She was born Susan Weston[2] in Edinburgh, and had trained at Marjory Middleton's Scottish Ballet School there before going on to the Royal Ballet School in London for two years. Her arrival in the company finally refuted recurring complaints in some quarters that Scottish dancers were being ignored, when in fact none had come forward with the requisite standard. She was followed a few months later by Anne Allan, and then by Ruth Prior, who is still with the Scottish Ballet, and the same year brought the company's first Scottish male dancer in the person of James Cameron from Arbroath, a student of William Mowat-Thomson in Edinburgh, although he remained for only a short time.

[2] British Actors' Equity rules forbid the same or similar names for two or more members, to avoid professional confusion.

"Whirlpool"   (Anthony Crickmay)

Touring activities were extended in 1970-71, first with the Scottish Arts Council's 'Stage One' scheme, which provided for fourteen weeks of opera, ballet and drama by the Scottish Theatre Ballet and six other companies in Glasgow, Edinburgh and Aberdeen in the Autumn of 1970, and then with a precursor of the later 'Ballet for Scotland' tours in February 1971. This took the company on one-night stands to smaller centres[3] with an enterprising programme for which Darrell created a new work, *Four Portraits*, and Walter Gore revived an earlier work, *Peepshow*. These were supplemented by Cranko's *Beauty and the Beast* Laverne Meyer's *The Web* and Bournonville dances from *La Ventana*. Before, during and after the tour, Glasgow performances were also given at the Close Theatre Club with a partly different programme that included Darrell's *Jeux* and Gore's *Street Games*, and then the company prepared its first major classic in Darrell's new approach to *Giselle*, which is described in Chapter 7. First performed at Aberdeen (His Majesty's) on 30 March, it was enthusiastically received and was toured during the following three months to Glasgow, Perth, Blackpool, Swansea, Sunderland and Manchester, in a repertory with Darrell's *Beauty and the Beast*. The latter also brought about the company's first appearance outside Britain, for two performances at the Zurich Festival in June.

The new season in September brought the appointment of Stuart Hopps as associate director, with the main task of extending the work of the company into schools and colleges. At the same time, the repertory for larger theatres was supplemented by a special programme, 'Background to a Ballet', devised by Harry Haythorne for matinée performances mainly given for schoolchildren. It comprised two parts, of which the first started with an introduction to the dancers and their daily routine, followed by a demonstrated commentary on the choreography, story, design and production of *Giselle*. After an interval, the instruments of the orchestra were introduced and the first act of *Giselle* was given a full performance. The programme had a wide success in introducing many hundreds of children to the principles and practical working of classical ballet.

Hopps now started plans for lecture-demonstration work in the schools themselves. He had a background of drama and modern dance rather than classical ballet: his *Sleepers* in the *Ploys* programme already mentioned was in fact his first work with classical dancers. He had, however, studied at the London School of Contemporary Dance when it first opened at The Place; had spent two years in the USA with an artist's award from the Arts Council of Great Britain, where he worked with outstanding personalities such as Martha Graham, Merce Cunningham, Alwin Nikolais, Paul Taylor and José Limón; had freelanced in musical theatre and television as a choreographer, and had taught dance at Dartington College in Devonshire.

In January 1972 Hopps put together a pilot programme at Notre Dame College in Glasgow which was shown to an invited audience of educationists from all over Scotland. It comprised an exploration of dance and movement involving student teachers from the College alongside six dancers from the company; a work intended for secondary school audiences performed by members of the company, and a discussion. The response was favourable, and Hopps went ahead with the genesis of 'Moveable Workshop', which began a year later, and in which classical ballet would be one among several elements in a dance experience related to work the children were doing, and involving them creatively. In the meantime, and in collaboration with George Reid of Scottish Television, Hopps gave the main company its first ballet on a specifically Scottish subject, *An clò Mor* (The Big Cloth), based on Gaelic songs and the ritual waulking of island tweed.

The ballet was a novel element in the 1972 Ballet for Scotland tour, contrasting with *Street Games*, Ashley Killar's *Journey* and the Bournonville dances from *William Tell* staged by Hans Brenaa. The tour opened

---

[3] The tour visited successively: Callander, Anstruther, Glenrothes, Duns, Hawick, Dumfries, Troon, Alloa, Motherwell, Dunoon, Kilmarnock, Greenock, St. Andrews, Forfar, Aberdeen (Arts Centre), and Invergordon.

with a week at Glasgow's Citizens' Theatre and another week at Dundee, but the schedule of sixteen other centres in three weeks had to be cut short because of industrial trouble in electrical supply. A pattern was now established of differentiating between the tours to major centres undertaken by the full company, and those to smaller centres with limited facilities, requiring fewer dancers and a different repertory. Back in Glasgow, there was special coaching from Dame Alicia Markova for *Giselle*, and a master-class she gave was recorded for television showing; the Friends of Scottish Ballet was formed on the enthusiastic initiative of Alison McLeay, its first honorary secretary, and the company as a whole was plunged into rehearsals for a new three-act ballet by Darrell, *The Tales of Hoffmann*.

This was first staged at the King's Theatre, Edinburgh, on 6 March, and was a success from the start (see Chapter 8); Leonard Salzedo conducted, and was appointed the company's principal conductor that year. The scale of the production

prevented it from being taken to Perth, where the company next went, but it was performed in Glasgow and Aberdeen, and in May it went south to Hull and Cardiff. There was another major production before the year was out, when Darrell made a start towards a complete *Nutcracker* by staging Act 2 alone, originally at York (Theatre Royal, 26 September), followed by other places in England and Scotland. Difficulties over the adequate fireproofing of the attractive 'smarties' set of suspended multi-coloured spheres, designed by Philip Prowse, meant that only part of it could be used on the tour.

Between these major undertakings the company's experimental work was further developed in *Tangents*, a programme first staged in Glasgow at the Close Theatre Club as part of the Clyde Fair International, and then taken to the Edinburgh Festival fringe (there being no hint of any official festival invitation, nor would there be for another five years). *Tangents* comprised four original works, of which Peter Cazalet's *Some Bright Star*, reflecting the strains and

Gordon Aitken in "Tales of Hoffmann"
(Anthony Crickmay)

40

stresses of virtuoso performers, was later taken into the touring repertory. Darrell related social comment to *musique concrète* (a taped collage made from everyday sounds) in *Variations for a Door and a Sigh*; Hopps made outrageous comedy in *Positively the Last Final Farewell Performance* from historical figures who had mysteriously disappeared, and in *Balkan Sobranie* the young modern-dance choreographer Richard Alston (who formed his London-based group, Strider, this year) worked with classical dancers for the first time.

Two more new ballets were staged as part of a 'Fanfare for Europe' gala at the King's Theatre, Glasgow (7 January 1973) attended by Prince and Princess Michael of Gloucester. These were an engaging diversion called *Fanfare for Europe 1973* by Toer van Schayk from Holland, and Darrell's dramatic duet, *Scorpius*, to music by Thea Musgrave. Following the Sunday-night performance, the company was due in London the next afternoon for a charity matinée at Drury Lane Theatre. With just twenty minutes from the end of the performance to the departure of the night train, the dancers were taken in full costume and make-up, with a police escort, to Central Station, where astonished passengers watched them scramble aboard in tutus, body-tights or, in one case, an Edwardian bathing-costume.

The next month brought the production of André Prokovsky's *Scarlatti and Friends* and Antony Tudor's *Soirée Musicale* for the Ballet for Scotland tour repertory, and the launching of the first Moveable Workshop educational programme, using nine dancers from the main company. This was devised by Remy Charlip, a former member of the Merce Cunningham company who taught children's theatre at Sarah Lawrence College, New York, and wrote and illustrated numerous children's books. He was engaged with the help of a special grant from the Calouste Gulbenkian Foundation, and his programme, called *Quick-change Artists*, was welcomed as 'a unique form of entertainment, in which the piece by piece building of dance compositions by dancers themselves is presented with skill, delightful informality and much amusement . . .

"Tales of Hoffman" with Peter Cazalet
(Anthony Crickmay)

Its appeal will be to anybody remotely interested in dance from any angle, for it manages to combine the qualities of a fast-moving revue with a fascinating lecture-demonstration of the evolution of dances from widely varied starting-points'.[4]

Quick-change Artists was first shown at Braidsfield School, Clydebank, on 1 February, and then taken to other schools and colleges in Edinburgh, St. Andrews, Stirling, Perth, Aberfeldy, Blairgowrie, Crieff and Aberdeen. Of the major cities, Glasgow was conspicuous by its absence, having declined to engage the group at all. Reasons given in remarks by an official of the Corporation's Education Department, as reported at the time, involved the question of 'value for money', and suggested that there must have been some extraordinary misunderstanding on the part of Education Department officials about the nature of the programme, its content and purpose.

Otherwise the work of the Scottish Theatre Ballet in its widest sense had brought it a popular reputation throughout the country, and phrases such as 'always a popular event' were appearing in local newspaper reports from year to year. To forge further links in this direction an appeal was made to each local authority in the centres visited by the company to supplement the central grant from the Scottish Arts Council, which had risen from the initial £93,000 in 1969-70 to £137,750 for 1972-73. The results of this appeal varied considerably. Edinburgh Corporation approved a grant of £3,000 but spread over two years. At the other extreme, Oban turned down proposals to give the company preferential terms for the hiring of a hall, or to donate £5, and settled instead for a subscription of precisely £2.[5] In the year as a whole, however, the support from local authorities in Scotland more than trebled to a total of £12,354, while the company earned £42,875 at the box office from 127 performances, which were seen by over 56,000 people.

As one newspaper comment put it at this time: 'One of the happiest and most successful ideas of the Scottish Arts Council in recent years was to invite Western Theatre Ballet to come north and establish themselves as a permanent full-time company under their new title of Scottish Theatre Ballet . . . So well have they succeeded that they return next week as familiar friends, and it is difficult to appreciate that STB took up residence at their Glasgow headquarters only in April 1970. How much poorer we would be without them'.[6] Changes in the board of directors had also brought stronger Scottish connections, including the appointment of Robin Duff, who succeeded Mrs. Hewer as Chairman in May. In the same month Muriel Large, who later became administrator of the Irish Ballet Company on its establishment as a nationally-funded company in Eire, was succeeded as administrator of STB by Robin Anderson. The two Robins have since remained key figures in the company's continuing development.

[4] Una Flett, *The Scotsman*, 9 February 1973.
[5] *Oban Times*, 15 February 1973.
[6] Alastair Selway, Aberdeen *Evening Express*, 4 May 1973.

6.
Progress

"The Dancing Floor" with Marian Spelshare and
Barry McGrath   (Anthony Crickmay)

Both Robin Duff and Robin Anderson had previous connections with ballet before they became, on 28 May 1973, Chairman of the Board of Directors and Administrator respectively of Scottish Theatre Ballet. Robin Duff is Laird of Meldrum since he inherited the family estates in 1954, where he now has a flourishing hotel. He had a long and continuing interest in ballet during a colourful earlier career in journalism and broadcasting, and his friendship with many of the leading personalities in British ballet has been one advantage of his chairmanship. He is very much an active Chairman, seldom missing a performance of interest or importance, concerned for the welfare of individual dancers and staff and understanding their problems. In addition, having given much of his time to public service work in local government, he has a firm control over the Chairman's duties.

Robin Anderson has already been mentioned as the very practical assistant who helped Veronica Bruce to launch her summer ballet festivals in Moray (see Chapter 2). He also did much work for Margaret Morris' Celtic Ballet, and acted as an occasional stage manager for Marjory Middleton's presentations in Edinburgh and for Catherine Marks in Glasgow. A Dunfermline man, he first qualified as a pharmaceutical chemist before deciding to seek a career in the theatre, and a road accident as a child, which left him with a permanent limp, brought about an interest in skating to strengthen the injured leg. This succeeded so well that he won the Scottish pair-skating championship. He took the course in arts administration introduced by the Arts Council, worked as manager of Leicester's Phoenix Theatre and, from 1971, as Administrator of the Harrogate Theatre before obtaining his present appointment — 'the job of a lifetime', as he called it.

Together with Peter Darrell they have channelled the company's hard work into a continuing line of progress: cultivating the roots already put down in Scotland by their predecessors; extending the prestige of the company and its dancers by tours abroad and the collaboration with international guest stars, and fighting the perpetual economic battle to bring about better conditions along with higher standards. They have organised the company's activities into a pattern of development year by year which has, since 1973, trebled both the number of performances and the size of audiences; wiped out an accumulated deficit, and quadrupled the income earned at the box-office — results reflected in the commensurate increase in Scottish Arts Council support from public funds (see table in the Appendix).

When Duff and Anderson took charge of the administration, the company had just completed a Spring tour to Bradford, Birmingham, Cardiff and Swansea, as well as the three major Scottish centres, performing *Giselle* and a triple bill. The latter consisted of *The Nutcracker* Act 2, Toer van Schayk's ballet from the 'Fanfare for Europe' gala, now renamed *Ways of Saying Bye-bye*, and a first production for Scotland of the Fokine classic, *Le Carnaval* (1910), which Elisabeth Schooling had previously taught to Western Theatre Ballet with help from one of the original cast: Tamara Karsavina, no less. In June a further workshop programme was given at the Glasgow University Union, the Close Theatre having just been severely damaged by fire. Seven ballets by members of the company were performed, and there was particular praise for Brian Burn's *Vivaldi plus 4* and a *Reverence to Rameau* by Harold King.

Peter Darrell absented himself for some weeks this summer, first to stage *The Tales of Hoffmann* in New York for American Ballet Theatre, one of the leading companies in the USA. He also undertook another commission, this one at Jacob's Pillow in Massachusetts, where the annual summer dance festivals, begun in 1942, are major events in the dance world. A star performer there in 1973 was Dame Margot Fonteyn, and Darrell choreographed a special solo for her to dance at the festival — an association which later had rewarding consequences for the Scottish company.

Still lacking any official invitation to the Edinburgh Festival, however, they again appeared as a 'fringe' event this year at the Gateway Theatre, where a new work by Jack Carter, *Three Dances to Japanese Music*, was the first ballet to receive one of the

special awards given by *The Scotsman* newspaper for original work on the fringe. The ballet (discussed in Chapter 9) shared an impressive programme which comprised the first revival since WTB days of Darrell's *Jeux* (1963), Maurice Béjart's *Sonate à trois* (1957) and Antony Tudor's *Soirée musicale* (1938). When this is set against an official festival policy which that year set up an expensive *ad hoc* opera company under a conductor (Daniel Barenboim) who had never conducted opera before and was therefore privileged to start learning at the festival's expense, I believe my own comment at the time was more than just-ified: 'In opera and ballet, the festival has its priorities all wrong in relation to the funds available'.[1]

The first two sections of Carter's ballet were included in a programme given earlier that month at Ochtertyre, where a small studio theatre was built in the grounds of the late Sir William Murray's estate near Crieff. Sir William was then one of the Scottish Ballet's Board of Directors, and members of the company took part in his first privately-financed Ochtertyre Festival held there in

1972, when they performed *An Clò Mor, Street Games* and classical excerpts. (A further visit occurred in 1974, when Princess Alexandra attended a performance given in a joint season with Scottish Opera. The project came to a tragic end when, without public or other funds to supplement his own, and depressed by the state of affairs of a little theatre that had attracted much interest and affection, Sir William took his own life.)

Before the end of 1973 two major product-ions were staged which have remained among the most successful in the repertory: *La Sylphide*, the nineteenth-century Bour-nonville classic with a Scottish setting, staged in authentic style by Hans Brenaa from the Royal Danish Ballet, and Darrell's completed production of *The Nutcracker* in time for the Christmas season at Edinburgh. Given at the Royal Lyceum Theatre instead of the King's, it was seen by more than 20,000 people and took £21,000 at the box-office, making it the company's most successful venture at that time. It also afforded the opportunity of guest artists

---

[1] *Dance and Dancers*, November 1973.

Anna McCartney in "Three Dances to Japanese Music" (Anthony Crickmay)

sharing the principal roles: Diana Vere and Gary Sherwood from the Royal Ballet, and the Canadian dancers, Anna-Marie and David Holmes, who alternated with the company's own principals.

Being less familiar through its music, *La Sylphide* took longer to win the public's enjoyment of its period character and charm, and at first there was some inevitable confusion between it and Fokine's one-act *Les Sylphides*, despite the seventy-five years that separated their original productions. The confusion was not helped by the fact that, whereas care is usually taken by managements and Arts Councils to avoid overlapping tours by subsidised companies, when *La Sylphide* was first taken to Sunderland, the touring company of the Royal Ballet were found to be appearing the same week in neighbouring Newcastle, with *Les Sylphides* in their repertory.

Both *La Sylphide* and *The Nutcracker* involve children dancing, and it is generally the practice to invite ballet schools in the areas visited by the company on tour to send their best pupils to audition for the stage roles. Competition is often keen, and the chance of appearing with a professional company is an incentive for school and teachers as well as for the children, whose participation also strengthens local interest in the performances. On the first tour of *La Sylphide*, however, it was decided to double-cast the young girl who features prominently in the ensemble dances, and to take the two chosen girls throughout, making the necessary arrangements for a chaperone to accompany them and for temporary schooling wherever they went. The distinction of being the first juvenile members of the company for such a tour consequently belongs to Seonaid MacLeod of Edinburgh, now an adult member of the company, who was fourteen at the time, and Roberta Moir of Clydebank, who was then aged ten.

To fill out the programme, the two-act *La Sylphide* was at first given a curtain-raiser in the form of *Embers of Glencoe*, by the distinguished Scottish-born choreographer, Walter Gore, with music for percussion alone by a fellow-Scot, Thomas Wilson. In spite of its Scottish subject it found little favour, and was later replaced by other works such as Carter's *Three Dances to Japanese Music*, which was successfully taken into the main repertory and performed

"La Sylphide" with Patricia Rianne and Barry McGrath   (Anthony Crickmay)

46

Marian St. Claire in "Three Dances to Japanese
Music"
(Anthony Crickmay)

many times at home and abroad. Harold King's Rameau ballet from the 1973 choreographic workshop was added to the Ballet for Scotland tour repertory in 1974 under the title of *Partie de Campagne*, and shared a programme which included a work of frivolous but entertaining Scottish allusions in *The Tartans*, Frank Staff's reproduction of a lighthearted 1930s divertissement by Ashton.

In the office shared by Peter Darrell and Robin Anderson there is a poster-photograph of Fonteyn on which she has inscribed: 'Dear Peter — It was you who made me do the tour, all my thanks. It has been wonderful. Love, Margot'. The poster is a precious souvenir of the company's tour of Australia and New Zealand, which occupied seven weeks in the Spring of 1974. Dame Margot danced in all forty-six consecutive performances, alternating *La Sylphide* with Act 2 of *The Nutcracker* in one programme, and dancing pas de deux from *Swan Lake* and Skibine's *Romeo and Juliet* in the other. She was partnered by Ivan Nagy, the Hungarian-born premier danseur

of American Ballet Theatre, with whom she has worked on many occasions. The repertory also included Act 2 of *The Tales of Hoffmann*, *Three Dances to Japanese Music* and *La Ventana*. Organised by the Australian impresario, Michael Edgley, the tour took the company to Perth, Melbourne, Adelaide and Sydney, and to Wellington and Dunedin in New Zealand.

The opening-night performance at Her Majesty's Theatre, Perth, on 25 March 1974 was also the first occasion that the company appeared under its new title of The Scottish Ballet. The board decided to drop the word 'Theatre' partly because of intentions in Scotland to set up a national theatre company for drama, and also because it was thought to be superfluous for a company now accepted as Scotland's national ballet. However, it was an unplanned coincidence that the first use of The Scottish Ballet at Perth, Western Australia, should have echoed the first appearance of the Scottish Theatre Ballet at Perth, Scotland, almost five years before. More significantly, the tour was an important milestone in bringing

"Tales of Hoffmann" Act 3   (Anthony Crickmay)

48

the company an international reputation, and a psychological boost to its members. While the bulk of Press attention inevitably centred on Fonteyn, the company as a whole was enthusiastically praised for its style and corporate standard, with particular bouquets for Marian St. Claire and Michael Beare, and for the New Zealand-born Patricia Rianne, who had a heroine's welcome in her native country.

Robin Anderson later declared that the company rose magnificently to every occasion and put in some stunning performances. He was glad that the tour broke theatre records in almost every city, and made a profit for its impresario, with a corresponding share for the Scottish Ballet itself: 'not quite solving Britain's trade deficit', as he put it, 'but putting a few pennies in our ballet pocket'. He found the tour well organised, and was delighted at the evident rapport between Fonteyn and the company. 'I think the seal on our relationship', he recalled, 'was set when, on the way out, we

had a wait of nearly four hours in Singapore for our connecting plane to Perth. Qantas had arranged a private room for her to retire to and when I sought her out to tell her, she said, ''No — I shall stay with the company''. And so she waited for all that time in a humid, crowded and noisy transit lounge with the rest of us. From then on she became one of the company'.

Although another planned tour with Fonteyn the same year to the Corfu Festival had to be abandoned because of the political situation which developed at that time, such happy relations bore further fruit the following November when she danced in Scotland for the first time in six years. She appeared in two Scottish Ballet gala programmes at Glasgow and Edinburgh, again with Nagy, and a year later Peter Darrell created for her *The Scarlet Pastorale*, which she premiered with the company at Edinburgh (21 October 1975) and afterwards performed at Glasgow, Aberdeen and Norwich.

Shortly before the Australian tour the board

Dame Margot Fonteyn, Augustus Van Heerden in "The Scarlet Pastorale"

49

(Anthony Crickmay)

appointed an Australian conductor, Gerald Krug, as the company's full-time musical director. Trained in Sydney and Paris, he had held a similar post with the Australian Ballet, as well as having been a principal conductor of the Australian Opera and a concert conductor of experience. He initiated the orchestral reorganisation, in the Autumn of 1974, whereby players were henceforth engaged from Scottish musical sources instead of through a London agency. Soon afterwards Krug resigned, and was succeeded in July 1975 by Terence Kern, musical director of the London Festival Ballet and a conductor of particular skill in dance, much admired by dancers themselves in Britain, South Africa, the USA and elsewhere. With the help of Allan Morgan as assistant conductor, and of Clive Thomas, who became orchestra manager early in 1976, Kern had a larger orchestra to direct. It first appeared as The Scottish Ballet Orchestra in March 1976, and is now maintained at a usual strength of 45—55 according to requirements. When Kern regrettably left in the Spring of 1977, Morgan continued as resident conductor until Bramwell Tovey, also from London Festival Ballet, became musical director in November 1978.

More progress was made in other directions. It was decided that future programmes for schools needed dancers with a special commitment, who could combine with the main company when necessary. Stuart Hopps accordingly formed Moveable Workshop, consisting of five dancers and a pianist, with their own technician and administrator, who would not only perform in schools but engage in workshop sessions with pupils. After collaborating with actors and musicians in *Columba*, a Christmas production at the Traverse Theatre, Edinburgh, they went out the following March on a nine-weeks tour. Besides special works by Hopps, the repertory included the first version of Darrell's *O Caritas*, a protest against senseless violence, with songs by Cat Stevens, which was later taken into the main repertory.[2]

During the same year, Moveable Workshop went 'overseas' for a tour of Northern Ireland as part of an Ulster Arts Festival embracing Queen's University, Belfast, and six other centres,[3] and in the Spring of 1975 it made a first visit to the Western Isles, where theatrical dance was an exotic commodity indeed. Among the works performed was Hopps' *An clò mor* with the Gaelic singer, Dolina MacLennan. According to the *Stornoway Gazette* (17 May 1975), it was given 'a rapturous welcome', and the report continued: 'At the end a voice from the hall called out, ' "Gle mhath a Dhollag". This was answered from behind the stage by a happy cry of "tapaidh leat!" '. Part of the success of the group was due to their involvement of the audiences to whom they performed, whether schoolchildren or adults, in what Una Flett in a *Scotsman* review (19 December 1974) called 'Not so much a programme as an exercise in flexible reactions'.

At Glasgow in November 1974 Harry Haythorne said farewell after a 25-year association with ballet in Britain that began when he came from his native Adelaide in 1949 to join Metropolitan Ballet. He became a ballet-master of distinction and an expert on dance notation, and as assistant to Peter Darrell he was invaluable and much-loved. The 'Introduction to the Ballet' programmes he began with the Scottish company were succeeded from 1975 by 'Prelude to the Ballet', a different venture but with a similar educational purpose, demonstrating the conventions of ballet and the training of dancers, with film and slide illustrations and a direct reference to the current repertory of the company. It was initiated by Donald McCulloch, who was appointed publicity and promotions manager in 1974, and who involved Jim Hastie, the present ballet-master for Scottish Opera and a speaker of persuasive charm. He devised a presentation which still operates successfully and is performed 30—40 times a year. It features one of the company's female dancers, who is put through the elements of a class and illustrations from the repertory, accompanied by Hastie's individual commentary, and with

[2] Moveable Workshop's first tour visited St. Andrews University, Ayr, Irvine, Aberdeen, Perth, Kinross, Dunblane and Alyth, as well as schools in Edinburgh and Glasgow.
[3] Londonderry, Newry, Omagh, Downpatrick, Ballycastle, Antrim.

Robin Haig and Paul Tyers in "O Caritas"
(Anthony Crickmay)

whom he demonstrates a classical pas de deux partnership in terms of what can go wrong as well as what it should be.

Touring by the main company expanded in 1975 with a first 'double tour' under the Ballet for Scotland arrangements, whereby the company divided itself into two smaller groups, each taking the same repertory to different centres simultaneously. By using smaller forces, with about sixteen dancers in each, and with piano or taped music where an orchestra cannot physically be accommodated, the scheme enables many more centres to be visited and a far greater area covered. It regularly involves some 5,000 miles in all on a typical tour, which may range from Brora and Thurso in the north to Dumfries in the south. Also in 1975 the dancers in training, students taking weekly company classes on a scholarship basis, were given the chance of public performance in their own programme, staged in Glasgow and Edinburgh and including works specially prepared for it, which has since become an annual event.

The Scottish Ballet made a contribution to the 1974 Edinburgh Festival, in the shape of dances choreographed by Darrell for the Scottish Opera production of Gluck's *Alceste*, but the company's own 'fringe' programme that year, comprising four new works, had to be cancelled when four dancers found themselves afflicted by injuries. The following year, still with no official festival engagement, the company decided to go it alone by giving an August season in Edinburgh immediately before the festival began. The gamble paid off handsomely. With a repertory of *Giselle*, *The Nutcracker*, *La Sylphide* and Jack Carter's *The Dancing Floor*, they played to over 80% of capacity at the King's Theatre — a total of more than 10,000 people, of whom a questionnaire showed 49% to be tourists. Small wonder that it was decided to make it three weeks the next year (in a joint season with Scottish Opera), and that further summer seasons have since been given there each year.

The first of several associations with

"The Dancing Floor" with Marian St. Claire and Barry McGrath   (Anthony Crickmay)

52

Rudolf Nureyev came about as a visit to Spain in September 1975, where they inaugurated Madrid's fourth International Dance Festival. Nureyev danced James in *La Sylphide*, and gave the premiere of *Moment*, by the American choreographer Murray Louis, created for him with four other male dancers, and using the String Quartet by Ravel. Nureyev also appeared for the first time in *Sonate à Trois* (with Elaine McDonald and Robin Haig), and in Flemming Flindt's *The Lesson*, and the company gave its first performance of Dolin's *Variations for Four* (1957). Spanish reviews praised the 'preparation and personality' of the company; the 'grace and dynamism' of the corps de ballet, and the class of their leading dancers which put them on a par with their 'princely guest'. A week in Madrid was followed by another in Barcelona, where they were also acclaimed and where Niels Kehlet from the Royal Danish Ballet was a welcome guest in *La Sylphide*.

As John Percival commented in a report for *Dance Magazine* (USA): 'A company that can offer, in successive months, new ballets for Rudolf Nureyev and Margot Fonteyn has a lot going for it'. The Scottish Ballet returned triumphantly from Spain for *The Scarlet Pastorale* with Fonteyn. During the week of its Edinburgh premiere, a curious printer's error in the Royal Ballet programmes at Covent Garden identified the orchestra for Mikhail Baryshnikov's first *Swan Lake* appearance there as 'the Orchestra of the Scottish Ballet' — and no announcement was made to correct it! The mistake had crept in from the previous week's performances at the Newcastle Festival, where the Royal Ballet on tour had made use of the Scottish Orchestra. But as *Dance and Dancers* remarked editorially (December 1975): 'to blame anyone other than the real perpetrators for the noises that came from the Covent Garden orchestra pit that night was unfair; perhaps the Scots should sue for libel'.

After the opening of the beautifully renovated Theatre Royal in Glasgow that October, the Scottish Ballet first appeared there on Christmas Day 1975 with a season of *The Nutcracker* and scored another box-

"Le Carnaval" with Hilary Debden, Harry Haythorne and Michael Beare

(Anthony Crickmay)

office success. Earlier in the month, a call from Dame Margot Fonteyn took Graham Bart half way round the world to Mauritius, to dance with her in a series of classical pas de deux, including *Le Corsaire*, in which she had previously only danced with Nureyev. Thereafter the company was busy with rehearsals for Darrell's new full-evening ballet, *Mary, Queen of Scots*. It was premiered at the Theatre Royal on 3 March 1976 and later taken on tour, including a season at Sadler's Wells Theatre in London. The ballet is discussed further in Chapter 8; most reviews found it over-long and over-complex in its first version, and although it was revised and shortened for the summer season at Edinburgh, the balance of form and content (for which the present writer's own scenario must share the blame) was still less than satisfactory.

There were two visits to London that year, the second being for part of the so-called 'Nureyev Festival' at the London Coliseum, where he was billed to dance every performance for six weeks. The Scottish Ballet joined him for the last two weeks with *La Sylphide*, plus *Moment* and *The Lesson*, and

although his marathon was interrupted by a foot injury for part of one programme it was otherwise achieved. The injury caused his withdrawal from Act 2 of *La Sylphide*, so that Sally Collard-Gentle, who returned to the company a few months earlier after more than a year with the Australian Ballet, found herself pursued by a different James in Act 2 from the one she had enticed in Act 1, Graham Bart having taken over from Nureyev after the interval. After the final performance, Nureyev was made a kind of honorary Scotsman with the presentation to him of full Highland dress in the Stuart tartan.[4]

Moveable Workshop, in abeyance after Stuart Hopps left in 1975 to take up a teaching post in London, was newly formed late the next year under the direction of Sue Weston, a Bournemouth-born dancer whose experience ranged from classical ballet to

---

[4] It is worth noting that some sort of balletic history was made at this time with four major theatres in London simultaneously featuring dance companies: Coliseum/Scottish Ballet; Palladium/Australian Ballet; Covent Garden/Royal Ballet; Sadler's Wells/Dance Senegal.

Gyula Harangozó in "Napoli"   (William Cooper)

cabaret. She had toured various countries in Europe, the Middle East and North Africa, and had staged dances for theatre companies and on television. Her schools programme, 'Chance Dancing', followed similar lines to the previous workshop in its combined purpose of performance plus involvement, and it first went on tour in January 1977 with Susan Cooper, Christopher Blagdon, Serge Julien, Greta Mendez and Sue Weston herself as the dancers. At the time of writing the first two are still with the Workshop, in a notably successful 1978-79 programme, *Wowza*. The Workshop policy is further discussed in Chapter 10.

Sue Weston said at the outset that the group would perform wherever it was physically possible, and this included a daily 'trailer' in a shop-window on Edinburgh's George Street when they were giving performances on the 1977 Festival fringe. Meanwhile the main company also pioneered new locations with *The UFO Show*, devised by Peter Darrell in the Autumn of 1976 specially for pub and restaurant performance. The ten dancers were somewhat bothered at first by the need to perform at close quarters with customers eating and drinking, but were generally well received at both lunchtime and evening performances.[5] Jim Hastie's 'Prelude to the Ballet' likewise broke new ground with a performance on British Rail's first high-speed train north of Edinburgh, and arrangements were even made to take it to an off-shore oil rig, with the intrepid Sally Collard-Gentle quite ready to be landed from a helicopter, when the authorities decided against it.

Potentially as dangerous for other reasons was the company's first Paris visit in February 1977, to appear in 'Le festival Nouréev', as it was billed, in the huge, unlovely and technically nightmarish Palais des Sports near the Porte de Versailles. Darrell said it was like 'a leap into the lion's jaws' to take a repertory based on *Giselle* and *La Sylphide*, both Paris ballets originally, even with Natalia Makarova dancing the title role in each of them and thereby

5 'Ballet and Beer'. *The Scotsman*, 15 November 1976.

Jim Hastie in Prelude to the Ballet

making her debut with the company. The French critics predictably concentrated on the stars, and exposed their provincialism by suggesting surprise that 'Les Ecossais' should do other than stick to their kilts. Professional opinion, however, in the person of the ballerina Violette Verdy, then Director-elect of the Paris Opéra ballet, highly praised the company's dancing as a whole. She commented: 'You feel that this is a company with a sort of compact unity and a character of its own'.[6]

It was at a matinée of La Sylphide on this visit that a column of sparks was seen to rise above the false proscenium when Nureyev was dancing a variation in Act 2. While one section of the audience leaped to its feet shouting 'Feu! Feu!', Terence Kern carried on conducting and Nureyev imperturbably went on dancing until the front curtain was drawn across and the performance temporarily halted. By this time backstage, Kenneth Saunders had found a hose and Gordon Aitken, in costume as Madge the witch, doused the fire. It started when a front-cloth, which would have been 'flown' upwards in a proper theatre but which here had to be wound sideways, wrapped itself round some stage lights and ignited from the fierce heat. Word was taken to Darrell and Robin Anderson in a bar across the road that the theatre was on fire. Asked what they did, Anderson commented: 'Well, we finished our drinks and went over'.

Back in Scotland, Darrell's new and original version of Swan Lake (see Chapter 7), the only production in Britain and most of Europe to mark the centenary of the ballet's premiere, was first staged at Edinburgh (23 March 1977) and then taken on tour. After a further summer season at Edinburgh the Scottish Ballet actually appeared in its own right at the official Edinburgh Festival for the first time, at the King's Theatre, staging not only La Sylphide but its first production of Les Sylphides as well. The latter was given in a triple-bill with Othello and The Scarlet Pastorale. The occasion brought Scotland its first sight of the spectacular Fernando Bujones of American Ballet Theatre, and of Makarova,[7] although she was then suffering from 'Taglioni's knee' (a 19th century balletic

euphemism for pregnancy), and Bournonville's Sylph was hardly a role to which she was ideally suited. Dance and Dancers commented editorially (September 1977) that the company was 'still thought by the Festival directors to need guest stars for a work in which its own dancers have been internationally acclaimed'.

At a Press conference during the Festival Robin Duff announced an appeal to provide permanent premises — studios, offices and storage space — for the company, negotiations for which were already in progress. They were completed in December with the purchase of the new headquarters at West Princes Street for £35,000. By the end of 1978 funds had already topped £200,000 towards a target of £230,000 needed to pay for the conversions as well, and there was an immediate saving in rent for the sixteen different Glasgow premises the company had otherwise required for one purpose or another.

When he announced the appeal, the Chairman commented that the ballet company's needs were modest compared to those of the opera, and added: 'It's the ballet that plays to full houses, despite the fact that opera costs four times as much to produce'. His remarks were confirmed when figures for the previous season's activity showed that, with double-tours of Ballet for Scotland the company played to wider audiences than Scottish Opera or the Scottish National Orchestra, yet received a smaller grant from public funds than either of these, a situation which still continues. Earnings at the box-office, including visits abroad, topped £250,000 for the second year running.

Local authority support for the Scottish Ballet continued to veer erratically from council to council. An attempt to rationalise a basis for grants to this and other enterprises in the arts and in social welfare was made by the Convention of Scottish Local Authorities (COSLA), who recommended minimum figures for each regional council

---

[6] Una Flett: 'Pas de deux at the Palais des Sports', The Scotsman, 7 February 1977.

[7] A more Scottish form of 'Mackarova' was bestowed on her by the Dundee Evening Telegraph and Post, 25 August 1977.

on a basis of ratios per thousand of the population served. By 1978 a lop-sided response was evident, with some regions, like Lothian and Tayside, giving much more than the COSLA figure, and thereby indirectly subsidising others, such as Grampian, which fixed its grant at half the COSLA figure. Throughout Scotland, the COSLA recommendations were based on ratios of £44.25 per thousand people to the Scottish National Orchestra, £19 per thousand to Scottish Opera, but only £5.55 per thousand to the Scottish Ballet, in spite of it reaching a wider and more numerous audience than the others.

Although Robin Anderson warned that a cutback in support would inevitably mean a reduction in performances (a situation which is again threatened in the company's tenth anniversary year), the Scottish Ballet has continued to maintain a busy schedule of over 300 performances a year in one form or another, and to extend its repertory. André Prokovsky mounted the fuller version of his plotless *Vespri* (1973) for the 1978 Spring tour, a ballet which had otherwise only been seen abroad (his former New London Ballet danced a reduced version), and the com-

pany's second full-length Bournonville classic, *Napoli,* was successfully staged by Poul Gnatt of the Royal Danish Ballet at Edinburgh on 2 August. It featured a popular new guest in Gyula Harangozó from the Hungarian State Ballet, who danced Gennaro to Elaine McDonald's Teresina.

Harangozó's permit to perform here carried a strict time-limit, which meant that Graham Bart was also seen as Gennaro later in Glasgow — his last major role before giving up dancing in favour of restaurant management. At the beginning of the year, however, the company acquired a new American male principal in Paul Russell, formerly with the Dance Theatre of Harlem, the first classical company in the USA to consist of black dancers only. There was a new guest in Galina Samsova when the company paid a two-day flying visit to the Santander Festival in August, its third visit to Spain.[9] Later in 1978 Linda Anning went

[9] The second Spanish visit was in September 1977 to San Sebastian, with St. Jean de luz and Biarritz in France. Natalia Bessmertnova and Mikhail Lavrovsky of the Bolshoi Ballet shared the San Sebastian programmes, but dancing only pas de deux from their own repertory.

Elaine McDonald presents a bouquet to Her Majesty Queen Elizabeth the Queen Mother

back temporarily to her native New Zealand, where she met with her fellow New Zealander Patricia Rianne, who had left the company on her marriage the year before: they shared leading roles in *The Sleeping Beauty* as a special production to celebrate the twenty-fifth anniversary of the New Zealand Ballet.

Recent years have seen a new kind of investment in the engagement of distinguished teachers and former dancers to give special coaching and master-classes. Dame Alicia Markova was the first and she was followed by John Gilpin in 1976 (he returned in 1979 too), and in 1978 by Cleo Nordi and then Svetlana Beriosova, who paid special attention to *Swan Lake*, which was being revived for the Christmas season when the planned new *Cinderella* had to be postponed for budgetary reasons (this is now intended for Christmas 1979). Beriosova said in a television interview that she had never had a more enjoyable experience or known a company with such a strong corporate personality. On 15 October Peter Darrell himself went briefly 'back to the boards' when he took part in a gala performance at the London Coliseum for the Paul Clarke Memorial Fund. He danced in Kenneth MacMillan's *Valse Excentrique* with Brenda Last, once of Western Theatre Ballet and now Director of the Norwegian National Ballet, and Gordon Aitken, who in August had been given a new status at the Scottish Ballet's Assistant Artistic Director.

A section of the company appeared at the London Palladium for the first time in November at the Royal Variety Performance, which was given a Scottish character in tribute to Queen Elizabeth the Queen Mother, the guest of honour. The Scottish Ballet danced the reel from *La Sylphide,* and when individual security passes were distributed for entry to the theatre, they were found to include one each in the names of Auguste Bournonville and Hermann Lövenskjold. Moreover, a Press handout from the Palladium, when the programme was first announced, referred to the 'Royal Scottish Ballet' — a solecism repeated without correction in every newspaper report, including *The Scotsman!* Yet they had all been anticipated in this respect by the *Strathspey Herald,* which on 28 April 1978 had reported on future plans of the 'Royal' Scottish Ballet.

That so premature a title did not cause offence was amply demonstrated when, on 22 March 1979, Queen Elizabeth the Queen Mother paid a special visit to Glasgow, formally to open the headquarters building and to attend *The Tales of Hoffmann* at the Theatre Royal. The building had, of course, been in increasingly busy use for more than six months, as successive parts of it were made ready, and a successful exercise in public relations first occurred the previous October, when up to forty members of the public at a time were invited, at £1 a head, to tour the building, watch a condensed class, rehearsal and small-scale performance, and talk with the dancers in the Green Room afterwards. It proved so popular that the 'Open House', as it was called, had to be given more repetitions initially and others since, so that many admirers of the Scottish Ballet now know for themselves how much more secure the company is with a properly equipped base from which to plan and work for the future.

7.
The Classic Ballets

Elaine McDonald as Giselle
(Anthony Crickmay)

E very ballet company serving a wide public has to come to terms with at least some of the nineteenth-century classics that audiences still delight to see. For Peter Darrell, the question of artistic approach has to be settled afresh in each case. The Bournonville ballets, for instance, preserved in a continuous tradition and seldom performed by other UK companies, are best given in versions as authentic as possible. Other ballets in more or less regular production elsewhere in the UK, such as *Giselle*, *The Nutcracker*, *Swan Lake*, have been given distinctive new versions for the Scottish Ballet through renewed reference to historical sources, reconsideration of the musical basis, and theatrical relevance, while preserving the spirit and choreographic character that made them classics in the first place.

Darrell had long wanted to produce *Giselle* when he decided this was the most feasible of the major nineteenth-century classics for the company to tackle first, in 1971. He believed it should be staged as a story ballet with a strong dramatic content and not just as a vehicle for the ballerina. To this end he swept away much of the misty sentimentality that had become attached to it, while keeping the choreography that had come to us in the notation brought from Russia by Nikolay Sergueyev, the régisseur of the Diaghilev company, in the 1930s: it was taught to the Scottish company by Joyce Graeme, formerly an outstanding Myrtha in *Giselle* and an authority on the Sergueyev productions. Darrell's version brought the background into sharper, clearer focus through a more naturalistic setting and sense of character on the part of all concerned, while the musical revision not only restored passages usually cut, and instead omitted all additions not by Adam, but was specially re-scored for an orchestra of fourteen players by Humphrey Searle, to relate more closely to the nature of the production as well as to help the practicability for touring.

At first it took a while for ears to become accustomed to the absence of the usual string 'cushion' in the orchestra, but it soon became apparent that the arrangement actively enhanced the visual character, with designs by Peter Cazalet in the manner of Altdorfer or Grunewald. Act 1 is a village square in the middle ages, where Berthe keeps the inn and her daughter Giselle is a serving wench. Hilarion is the rough but honest suitor for Giselle, and Albrecht a suave ladies' man, rather mistrusted by the villagers. The ducal party arrives at the inn to watch a village festival at which the tragedy occurs. In Act 2 the Wilis, instead of appearing merely as decorative wraiths, are sinister washed-out shades of their former selves, nearer to Gautier's conception (it might be recalled, too, that the Wili was once equated with the Vampire in German folklore).

The musical revisions bring other changes. Act 1 loses the Burgmüller music for the Peasant Pas de deux, but a different pas de deux has been incorporated into the pas des vendanges instead. Giselle loses the two extra solos, one in each act, which the role acquired at some point during Petipa's late nineteenth-century productions in Russia, but instead she has a more extended Mad Scene to culminate in her suicide.[1] Elaine McDonald, the company's first Giselle in this production, confessed to problems with the role at first, in order to convince herself that a girl could really feel suicidal about being jilted, but found that modern theories of neurosis offered a way through to such a character.

Elaine McDonald accordingly became the first ballerina in Britain to vary the accepted portrait of Giselle as a very special girl, set apart from the rest and to some extent doomed from the start. This approach was initiated and exquisitely danced by Alicia Markova in the 1930s. The Giselle envisaged by Darrell and strongly embodied by McDonald is a very ordinary village girl, simple and rather gullible, but forceful enough to get angry with Albrecht when the truth begins to come out, and then to become mentally unbalanced by the shock of realisation. A performance of dramatic purpose as well as choreographic style, it was no doubt helped by her experience of

---

[1] It has always seemed to the present writer essential that Giselle should be seen to take her own life, as she does in this version, otherwise there is no reason for her grave to be in unconsecrated ground in the forest.

psychological character in Darrell's previous works for Western Theatre Ballet. McDonald has since become a ballerina of international calibre comparable to, say, Galina Samsova and Lynn Seymour, but whose loyalty to one company has perhaps prevented a wider recognition of her artistic stature.

*   *   *

The Nutcracker was begun in 1972 with Act 2 alone and not completed until the Christmas season of 1973. It reflects Darrell's awareness that this is as much a ballet for tomorrow as it has long been a classic of yesteryear, because more children make their first acquaintance with classical ballet through this than through any other work. Beneath its surface charm and simplicity it consequently bears a considerable responsibility for developing the adult audiences of the future — an aspect sometimes overlooked in its presentation. Darrell's approach is to present it primarily as a children's entertainment, but one addressed to a young audience of today

rather than some moist-eyed reminiscence of what children might once have been. The choreography and production make engaging use of both children and adults in performance.

The Christmas party of Act 1 is firmly placed by Philip Prowse's designs in a well-to-do nineteenth-century household. It is evidently some garrison town, as the Councillor von Stahlbaum of the original narrative has become simply 'the Colonel', and the male parents among the party guests share the same regimental uniform. Drosselmeyer retains his name but appears as a magician and conjuror with three exotically-garbed entertainers, whom Clara's dream later transforms into the Snow Queen, the Sugar-plum Fairy and the Nutcracker Prince. Their short solo dances at the party, as well as their costumes, ingeniously foreshadow the character and style of their later roles and so act as a recognisable link with the later scenes.

The sequence of events follows the fairy-tale basis, adding novel features that help towards a sense of enchantment for the

"The Nutcracker" Act 2   (Anthony Crickmay)

"The Nutcracker" with Sally Collard-Gentle and
Paul Russell   (William Cooper)

watching children. The Snow Queen, for instance, is flanked by two large and appealing polar bears who take charge of Clara; the Snow Queen is given a romantic pas de deux with the Prince in Darrell's most classically elegant style. The wordless children's chorus during the Snowflakes Waltz is embodied as two groups of costumed carol singers with their lanterns, on either side of the stage. Act 2 is a confection of visual delight with a setting of hundreds of multicoloured spheres suspended against black drapes, like a profusion of sugar-coated sweets. The character dances in the divertissement have all been re-thought afresh; they include a pas de quatre of small children unwrapped from a chocolate-box in the 'Mother Gigogne' number. The Grand Pas de deux keeps its Ivanov choreography, but after the sleeping Clara is discovered back in the original scene, and is carried to bed clutching her Nutcracker doll it is Drosselmeyer who has the last word. He bursts through the curtains with a flourish of his cloak as if to indicate that Clara's entire dream was his own biggest and best conjuring trick.

There were no musical revisions on the scale of *Giselle*, but an arrangement 'for small orchestra' of the Tchaikovsky score was at first made by Leonard Salzedo (who conducted the initial performances); both this and *Giselle*, however, are now performed in their original full orchestrations.

* * *

Swan Lake in 1977 underwent more substantial changes, without becoming the 'Swan Loch' that some had predicted and, perhaps, had hoped for. It was the only new production in Britain during the centenary year of the ballet's original Moscow premiere, and Darrell's new dramatic approach enabled the music to revert to its original 1877 sequence as Tchaikovsky composed it. At the same time, it retained the surviving choreography from the Petipa and Ivanov version of 1895 from which most productions in Western Europe have descended. This was skilfully staged by Sheila Humphreys in relation to Ivanov's choreography for the Lakeside scenes, and to Petipa's for the Act 1 pas de trois and the erstwhile 'Black Swan' pas de deux. This last, which Petipa shifted to Act 3, here

"Swan Lake" Act 3   (Anthony Crickmay)

Noriko Ohara and Nigel Spencer in "Swan Lake"
(William Cooper)

reverts to the music's original place in the first act; its place in the Ballroom scene of Act 3 is taken by the supplementary pas de deux Tchaikovsky composed at the request of Sobeschanskaya when she took over the central role at the ballet's fifth performance.

All this is possible because the basis of the story is no longer a bevy of bewitched maidens and an evil magician, but the tragedy of Prince Siegfried, who is corrupted and destroyed by the machinations of his friend Benno, now transformed into a sinister, Iago-like figure, replacing Rothbart. It is Benno who, in Act 1, brings Odile to the Prince's birthday-party and dances the 'Black Swan' pas de deux with her to display her dazzling beauty, captivating Siegfried. It is also Benno who introduces the Prince to the delights of opium-smoking, whereby Odette materialises, with her swans, as the ideal love of his pipe-dreams. The designs, again by Peter Cazalet, are in a conventional Victorian Gothic style, but done with an eye to dramatic character. As Darrell wrote in a programme-note: 'I attempted to retain the essence of the original plot — deception, true love against profane but setting it in the mid-19th century where young ideals are opposed to the moral strictures of the time'. This is stressed in the Ballroom scene, where the visiting princesses dance the character dances with their respective retinues, but Siegfried has eyes only for Odile, who is angrily rejected as a potential bride by the Queen Mother.

It also enables the Ballroom scene to be followed by the final Lakeside scene without a further interval, as I am sure Tchaikovsky intended. This is done by way of the Entr'acte he provided, which covers the scene-change, and a brief episode during which Siegfried is seen returning to his room and taking up his opium-pipe again. No longer is it the sad plight of the bewitched Odette which is the ballet's emotional fulcrum, but that of the bemused Siegfried in his desire for an ideal but unattainable love (rather like James in *La Sylphide*). His frustration drives him to stab himself, as Odette once more appears, grieving but beyond his reach.

At the initial performances in Edinburgh the dual role for the ballerina, with Odette as the mirror-image of Odile, was alternately danced by Elaine McDonald and Patricia Merrin, who came north from London Festival Ballet as a principal of assured technique and warm personality. Graham Bart, whose retirement in 1978 was surely premature for a dancer of his strong, muscular image, moved easily between the dashing Prince in one cast and a menacing Benno in another, with Paul Tyers the romantically tortured alternate Prince, and Cristian Addams the more insidious Benno.

Unlike the Russian choreographer Vladimir Bourmeister, whose newly-choreographed *Swan Lake* in 1953 was the first in recent times to revert to the original musical sequence,[2] Darrell's change of dramatic outline enabled him to have the best of both musical and choreographic worlds. He is able to retain what is known to be the most impressive contributions of both Petipa and Ivanov at the same time as he gives Tchaikovsky the tribute of respecting the composer's musical intentions, with a consequent gain in musical continuity and key-relationships in performance. This *Swan Lake* is a production of major significance for ballet which deserves to be seen in relation to more conventional versions, but although it was performed on tour in England at Hull, Southsea and Wolverhampton in 1977, it is a matter of regret that difficulties of funding have, at the time of writing, prevented it from being seen in London.

* * *

Among other nineteenth-century classics an obvious choice for the company was *La Sylphide*, in which the Scottish setting of the story is itself an acknowledgment, by one of the most celebrated of Romantic ballets, of the debt the Romantic movement in its wider aspects owes to Scotland as a source of fable and fancy. The ballet underwent a sex-change from its literary source: a story by Charles Nodier, *Trilby*, in which the wife of a Scottish fisherman is tempted by a handsome male sprite. In Adolphe Nourrit's scenario for the first ballet, by Filippo Taglioni for his daughter Marie at Paris in

[2] Another version using the music as originally composed was Jack Carter's for Buenos Aires and the London Festival Ballet in the 1960s.

1832, it became a Scottish farmer tempted from his fiancée by a sylph of the glen; in the end he loses both his real and his illusory love. Bournonville retained this narrative for his Copenhagen production in 1836 with Lucile Grahn, and with a new score by Hermann Lövenskjold, which is the version that has come down to us virtually intact through the continuing tradition embodied in the Royal Danish Ballet.

It was Hans Brenaa, a former member of the Danish company and an acknowledged authority on the Bournonville repertory, who taught the choreography and staged *La Sylphide* for the Scottish Ballet. Darrell had previously invited him to work with Western Theatre Ballet, for whom he staged the one-act *La Ventana* in 1968, which then became the first work the Scottish Theatre Ballet performed on its arrival in Scotland.[3] This was followed by two more Bournonville excerpts: the suite of dances from Rossini's opera, *William Tell*, in 1970, and the pas de deux from *Flower Festival at Genzano* in 1973. By the time the company came to *La Sylphide* later in 1973, therefore, the dancers knew something of the Bournonville style and technique which constitutes such a distinctive element of the wider classical heritage.

Although *La Sylphide* had been seen in London on visits by the Royal Danish Ballet, it had never become part of the regular repertory of any British company, except briefly in a production by Ballet Rambert in 1960-61 when that company was still classically-based. Consequently Darrell was wise to insist on retaining all its period charm and character, as well as the authentic choreography, to which the dancers rose admirably. This was notably apparent in the light, buoyant steps for the male principals (by which Bournonville helped to maintain the prestige of the male dancer on a par with the ballerina, and thereby distinguished the nineteenth-century Danish school from all other European styles in which the ballerina established her ascendancy).

Their success was complemented by the designs of Peter Cazalet, whose costumes and settings — a stone-built farmhouse for

[3] See Chapter 3.

"Dances from William Tell" (Anthony Crickmay)

Act 1, and a view of the glen from a tree-shaded clearing in Act 2 — achieved, with Molly Friedel's lighting, 'quite possibly the best-looking *Sylphide* of all time'.[4] It has sufficient naturalistic detail to be convincing, yet not to submerge the dance element by overblowing the setting into Scottish baronial proportions. Indeed, the relatively small scale of the production, partly determined by the stages on which it would be given, actively works to the ballet's advantage in intimacy of mood and sharpness of character. This is further underlined by the responsiveness of one character to another and the permutations of cast that involve individual dancers in more than one role, and an arrangement of the music for a small orchestra has now been replaced by the same orchestration the Royal Danish Ballet uses.

Alternate casts ensured a constant freshness and vigour in performances that captivated audiences from the start. In the first run the Sylphide was personified by Sally Collard-Gentle, shy and touchingly forlorn; Patricia Rianne, dramatic and seductive; and Marian St. Claire, delicate and precise. James was danced with bearded geniality by Cristian Addams, with Byronic intensity by John Fletcher, and with forthright yet sensitive feeling by Michael Beare. Fletcher also shared the role of Gurn with Bruce Steivel and Brian Burn, and the practical-minded Effie was divided between Amanda Olivier, Keri Stewart and Anna McCartney. Madge the witch, traditionally a male character role, was given a cold malevolence by Gordon Aitken, bibulous anger by Harry Haythorne, and aggressive intent by Gavin Dorrian.

*   *   *

More Bournonville followed five years later, in 1978, when the Scottish Ballet became the first British company to stage the three-act *Napoli*, some twenty-five years after the Royal Danish Ballet introduced it to London at Covent Garden. Since then the divertissement from the last act, a pas de six, had been performed from time to time by both companies of the Royal Ballet, and by London Festival Ballet, but in spite of the

[4] John Percival. *Dance and Dancers*. December 1973.

"Napoli" Act 1   (William Cooper)

generally favourable reception whenever the ballet was given in London, all the companies had fought shy of staging it as a whole. The Scottish Ballet engaged as producer Poul Gnatt, another experienced Bournonville dancer from the Royal Danish Ballet, who had grown up with *Napoli*, as it were, from being one of the watching children in Act 3 to dancing principal roles as an adult.

Once again it was Peter Cazalet whose designs, lit this time by John B. Read, gave visual appeal to a rather more tortuous tale involving a Neapolitan fisherman, Gennaro, and Teresina, his bride, whom he carelessly loses overboard during a storm, but successfully rescues from a watery fate among the nereids by the power of his love and faith. No less than four composers contributed the music for this: Gade, Helsted, Lumbye and Paulli, so that authenticity is more problematical in the music and its arrangement than in the choreography. The Scottish Ballet uses an orchestration commissioned for the Danish company by Harold Lander while he was its director, instead of the simpler version preferred by the late King Christian IX because he liked to conduct it himself, and still apparently retained in Copenhagen.

A strong case can be made for the fuller version in the ballet context, because the music has to carry the main weight of emotional expression and colour. Much of the ballet is more in the nature of a mime-play with dancing, the narrative mime being dependent on the music to give it character and feeling, as well as to clarify its intentions in some episodes. The dancing is concentrated in particular passages, such as the *ballabile* in Act 1, the dances of the underwater nereids in Act 2, and the well-known divertissement in Act 3. This last contains interpolated solos by Hans Beck, who made his debut with the Royal Danish Ballet two days before the death of Bournonville in 1879; he was responsible for continuing the Bournonville tradition into the present century, and for advising Lander on his major revivals in Copenhagen.

As these words are written, *Napoli* has had scant time to settle itself in the repertory, but its initial performances were distinguished by the guest appearance of Gyula

Harangozó from Budapest as Gennaro, with Teresina alternately portrayed by the romantically playful Elaine McDonald and the more insistently determined Patricia Merrin. Gennaro was also danced by Graham Bart, and by David Ashmole on a guest appearance from the Royal Ballet. A novel interpretation was given to the sea-sprite Golfo, who rules over the nereids in Act 2, by the almost reptilian quality the character acquired from Paul Russell, from the Dance Theatre of Harlem, in his first season with the Scottish company.

8.
The Darrell Ballets

"Five Rückert Songs" with Elaine McDonald
(William Cooper)

It has been a continuing policy for the Scottish Ballet to perform a high proportion of new works, and no less than nineteen have been created by Peter Darrell since the company became based in Scotland. These range from short *pièces d'occasion* to three full-length ballets, two of which had original music composed for them. The first was *Beauty and the Beast* (1969), with a score by the Scottish composer Thea Musgrave. This can be seen as something of a foundation-work for the company in drawing together many threads of Darrell's previous experience, and demonstrating his intentions for the future. His fluent choreographic blend of dance and drama was already evident in the works he had created for Western Theatre Ballet — some of which, such as *Jeux* (1963) and *Ephemeron* (1968), were to be seen again in the Scottish repertory — and much more had been learned from his first full-length ballet, *Sun into Darkness*, which WTB staged in 1966.

At the time this was a valiant attempt at something new in British ballet: an extended work on a contemporary theme, with music specially composed for it, and the collaboration of several talents.[1] The result had considerable balletic skill and immense theatrical effect, but an over-lurid theme, involving cruelty and perversion during a carnival ritual in a Cornish village, led to a coarseness of expression and told against its success, while its choreographic structure had some weak aspects. *Beauty and the Beast* benefited from this experience. Discussing the latter before its premiere, Darrell declared: 'I wanted to get away from lust, rape and murder for a change . . . I wanted to do a romantic work and I wanted to do a fairy story which had no fairies in it'.[2]

In the same interview he also acknowledged that as he grew older his choreographic outlook was becoming more classical, and that while he admired modern dance enormously he also believed that the classical vocabulary could and should be expanded. *Beauty and the Beast* put these precepts into effect, on the basis of a scenario by Colin Graham which went back to the original story by Madame de Villeneuve, and of a score by Thea Musgrave which was conceived in terms of its

theatrical purpose, and altered or modified as the ballet developed. It was composed for twenty players, to make it practicable for touring as well as suitable for different kinds of theatre; instrumentally balanced to register in association with a stage performance, and supplemented by a pre-recorded tape to intensify the supernatural element.

The tape came about as a result of a suggestion in the scenario for 'peals of wicked laughter', but as well as these being duly represented, the device was extended to provide an extra aural dimension associated both with the enchanted domain of Azor (the Beast), and with the idea of time-travelling by Rosaline (Beauty). Besides naturalistic representations of tolling bells, rushing winds and the like, the electronics are an extension of the orchestra and related to it as part of the composition, not merely superimposed as a sound-effect. Combined with the designs by Peter Minshall, which give the enchanted characters and their settings a metallic sheen shadowed (as the story is) by their own overtones, the world of Azor seems to acquire a kind of 'reality', while the scenes involving Rosaline's family suggest more of artifice or caricature.

Darrell's choreography is a classical dance narrative of skill and poetry, with clearly recognisable dance personalities for Rosaline and Azor: successive pas de deux reflecting their developing relationship, and scenes of other formal dancing as well as character dancing, all in a smooth flow from one to another. The ballet gave a rewarding role to the Vancouver-born Donna Day Washington, who had studied at both the School of American Ballet in New York and the Royal Ballet School before joining WTB in 1964. Her Rosaline, with its Cinderella-like pathos, innocence and vulnerability as well as assured classical technique, was her last and in some ways most memorable achievement before she retired for domestic reasons the following year, at the peak of

---

[1] Besides Darrell, *Sun into Darkness* was the work of David Rudkin (scenario), Malcolm Williamson (music), Harry Waistnage (design) and Colin Graham (production).

[2] 'On Creating Beauty — and Beasts', *Dance and Dancers*, November 1969, which also includes interviews with the other collaborators, expressing their intentions and describing their methods in detail.

her career. Azor was incisively danced by Tatsuo Sakai, a Japanese dancer of elegant style as well as exotic appeal.

We tend to think of a ballet as finished once it has been premiered, but Darrell is never afraid to make changes if he believes these will improve it, or to discard a work altogether if it is less than successful and not susceptible to revision. Within a few months some changes were made to *Beauty and the Beast:* an apotheosis at the end was abandoned, as were some divertissement dances; comic interludes were trimmed, and the final pas de deux was modified so that it expressed a longer and more sustained line. All these were to the general advantage of a ballet now certainly overdue for revival. It is unlikely, however, that we shall again see Darrell's next work, *Herodias* (1970), which suffered from some confusion of content and character although showing a characteristically inventive approach to a familiar story.

It involved a much-publicised portrait of Salome by a male dancer, in order to emphasise a pre-pubescent non-sexuality of character. The role was finely taken by Kenn Wells, who showed a remarkable facility for walking on his hands, after the manner of mediaeval woodcuts illustrating the Biblical character. There was also a double identity for Herodias old and Herodias young, as she 'meditates on her past life and relives the events by which she has achieved power'. Verses from Mallarmé's poem, *Hérodiade,* were translated into English and put into the mouths of some dancers as well as on tape, and the music by Hindemith was a score composed in 1944 for Martha Graham's ballet, *Mirror Before Me,* which the composer conceived as an orchestral parallel to Mallarmé, not as a setting of the words. All this had striking designs by Peter Docherty that owed something to Klimt as well as to Bakst, and a compelling dramatic personality by Elaine McDonald as the aged Herodias, grotesquely bloated, but the choreographic invention lacked a clear balletic focus for such a variety of elements: 'an exotic bloom — quite possibly carnivorous', as Clement Crisp described it in his review for *The Financial Times.*

"Beauty and the Beast"   (Anthony Crickmay)

Hilary Debden in "Beauty and the Beast"
(Anthony Crickmay)

For some time after this Darrell was mainly concerned with the company and its dancers, with getting the balance right and raising standards, and with adding works by other choreographers. He did create *Four Portraits* for the SAC tour in February 1971, but his choreographic imagination next reflected the unabashed entertainer in him with a three-act ballet that brought the company a major popular success, *The Tales of Hoffmann* (1972). It was an astute choice at this point: Offenbach's music was high among classical favourites, and the story of a poet's three disastrous love-affairs, framed by a prologue and epilogue involving a fourth, could just as well be danced as sung, given suitable simplification in some respects and amplification in others.

This time Darrell prepared his own scenario on the basis of the libretto Barbier and Carré wrote for Offenbach. Some lesser characters he discarded (Nicholas, Coppelius, Peter Schlemil), and Hoffmann is first seen as an elderly man mulling over souvenirs: a pair of spectacles, a ballet-shoe, a cross. He is persuaded by his drinking-companions to tell the stories that lie behind them, and these ingeniously reflect his changing personality: as a young man he is bewitched by a pretty face (Olympia); slightly older, he is fascinated by an artist (Antonia); in the Venice scene he becomes a middle-aged voluptuary at the sight of Giulietta. By the epilogue, however, although his fame has made him attractive to Stella, he is past responding and Lindorf, the incarnation of all his antagonists and rivals, has his final triumph.

Throughout the ballet Darrell's choreography attracts and holds the interest with a fund of fluent invention, rich in romantic character and with plenty of unforced humour. There is abundant vitality right from the prologue, with its bravura solos for three male dancers, Hoffmann's friends, and the start of Act 1 has an amusingly quirky pas de trois for Spalanzani and his two assistants as they assemble their doll piece by piece. What opera-goers know as the 'Doll Song' becomes a coloratura dance instead, and in the first cast Hilary Debden not only made much of the bravura steps but

"Tales of Hoffman" Act 2   (Anthony Crickmay)

also suggested that winsome charm beneath Olympia's hard surface, which Hoffmann supposedly sees through the magic lenses Spalanzani gives him. Instead of a singer, Antonia in Act 2 is a would-be ballerina, with Hoffmann as an encouraging partner; Marian St. Claire portrayed her with spirit as well as style, as Elaine McDonald did the glamorous Giulietta who presides over the sensual decadence of Dapertutto's Venetian salon.

Hoffmann's four ages of a poet calls for a corresponding range of character sustained on a firm basis of classical technique, which is most strongly tested as the partner for Antonia. His four-fold adversary (Lindorf, Spalanzani, Dr. Miracle, Dapertutto) is a rewarding role for expressive mime and character dance. Originally these male principals were strongly created by Peter Cazalet and Gordon Aitken respectively. Alastair Livingstone's designs give the spectacle a picturesque pantomime appeal, and John Lanchbery's 'arrangement' of Offenbach is as ingenious and successful as his version of Herold for Ashton's La Fille mal Gardée. Lanchbery raided other sources of Offenbach as well as the opera, and worked them all into a sequence of thematic associations and transcriptions which are almost a new score; only the Barcarolle theme is perhaps repeated once too often.

Darrell now entered on a creatively prolific period, in both large and small works. Tangents, a late-night programme for the Clyde Fair International and the Edinburgh Festival Fringe, included Variations for a Door and a Sigh (1972). This was a return to sharp social commentary in association with a sound-collage, by Pierre Henry, in which the creaks and sighs dictated something of the choreographic character. The two pairs of dancers involved are shown as seeking the novelty of changing relationships, first with different partners among themselves, and ultimately in direct communication with members of the audience, some of whom found themselves bound at the end in ropes brought on by an enigmatic goddess-figure, silver-bodied and platform-soled.

That relationships are compounded of love and hate in different proportions was dramatically conveyed in Scorpius (1973), a short but forceful duet based on the astrological proposition that those born under the sign of Scorpio make dangerous partners for each other. Patricia Rianne, a New Zealand dancer of sinuous style and dramatic personality, who joined the company on its move to Scotland (she was previously with Ballet Rambert), was seen to powerful purpose in the work's opening solo, and in the subsequent duet-dances with Brian Burn. The close-packed choreographic line achieved a compelling interest in the course of its relatively short span: a duration defined by the musical choice of Thea Musgrave's Chamber Concerto No. 1 for nine instruments. This helped to sustain the balletic tension so strongly that I feel the work should have had — and might still have — a more continuing place in the repertory.

A duet of a very different kind was the Grand Pas Gitane (1974) — a showpiece of classical bravura in which flamboyance is taken to the brink of satire. To music by Saint-Saëns, with some assistance from Romualdo Marenco, it was danced with such dazzling effect in the first instance by Marian St. Claire and Michael Beare that it earned from one critic, not himself an addict of French cigarettes, the ultimate comment: 'Every performance should carry a Government health warning'.[3] Darrell had his own warning to communicate, against the senselessness of violence in human affairs, in O Caritas (1974), which has a deceptively lightweight opening in a jazz style reminiscent of the choreographer's earlier work for a television programme, 'Cool for Cats', but which soon becomes serious in association with eight songs sung by Cat Stevens. George Wilkie's photo-projections of scenes of violence comprise the only decor. The ballet was first made for the company's small workshop group, but it was later added to the main repertory, where Paul Tyers, Leicester-born and Royal Ballet School trained, made his individual mark with an outstanding study in tragic disillusionment, and the clarity and directness of the choreography in general achieved an eloquent poetry.

3 Clement Crisp, The Financial Times.

Elaine McDonald and Frederick Jahn Werner in
"Grand Pas Gitane"   (Jim Wilson)

After *Voyage*, a solo for the Canadian dancer, Anna-Marie Holmes, in return for her several distinctive guest appearances in other roles, and a work to display students from the Saturday classes to Mendelssohn's *Songs without Words* (both 1975), Darrell rose to the challenge of another guest artist later that year with *The Scarlet Pastorale* for Dame Margot Fonteyn. Derived from Aubrey Beardsley and *The Yellow Book*, it gave Fonteyn an unusual double role in showing her initial image of purity as merely a façade for a thoroughly wicked nature underneath. It also plunged her into an ambience of sophisticated decadence not often associated with her balletic character, in which she not only expressed a persuasive lasciviousness but, in a splendid *coup de théâtre* at the very end, suddenly turned murderess when she sat up and throttled the nobleman who thought he had strangled her.

For this most unusual role Fonteyn had recommended a partner new for her (and her audiences) in Augustus van Heerden, then from the Boston Ballet. His mulatto appearance was particularly apt to his role of a strangely corrupt innocence. The effect was vividly enhanced by Philip Prowse's designs in the style of Beardsley, for which Fonteyn instinctively found a corresponding line of sharp-featured movement in Darrell's choreography (the role was later danced with comparable success by Elaine McDonald and Andrea Durant). The theatrical possibilities of the Swiss composer Frank Martin's ponderously-titled Concerto for Seven Wind Instruments, Strings and Percussion, first explored by Kenneth MacMillan in *The Burrow* (1958), were newly engaged by Darrell in terms of the music's contrasts of colour, texture, mood and rhythm (there is even a built-in musical parallel to the ballet's dramatic end-twist).

Darrell has always maintained that his choreographic ideas come out of the music — the sound, the rhythm and the feel of it — rather than finding music to fit ideas, as some choreographers do. Which is perhaps why he has been readier than most to work with original music — when a subject can be decided sufficiently far in advance to give

Dame Margot Fonteyn and Anthony Dowell in
"The Scarlet Pastorale"   (Anthony Crickmay)

the composer time to work. This happened with *Beauty and the Beast,* and it became practicable again for *Mary, Queen of Scots* (1976), in which Darrell showed that a historical subject close to the hearts of all Scots could be presented in balletic terms. The music was commissioned from John McCabe, the Liverpool-born composer and concert pianist, who had previously composed a score for Suzanne Hywel in *The Teachings of Don Juan* (Northern Dance Theatre, 1973), and Peter Docherty was engaged as designer.

It was at this point that Darrell decided a scenario would help to condense history and focus ideas, both for the composer and himself, and invited the present writer to prepare it. The challenge was exciting, and a collaboration developed as close, I believe, as that for *Beauty and the Beast* earlier. My first draft proposed that Mary's story should be told in flashback scenes from her captivity in England before her execution, but the choreographer preferred the chronological sequence we adopted. Each scene is planned to show Mary in a different relation-

ship to the men in her life, and she is also brought into unhistorical confrontation with Elizabeth I of England by the theatrical devices of a masque in one instance and a divided stage in another. After three or four revisions, a scenario of seven scenes was divided into two acts, and the episodes were timed so that each act would have a duration of 55—60 minutes.

In performance this became extended by the continuous musical structure for each act, which involved linking passages for the music to move from one dance to another. Some cuts were made after the initial performances, but it is entirely my own opinion that the musical conception prolonged the narrative and slowed-up the dramatic pace, as well as allowing no respite or breathing-space for an audience to absorb an unfamiliar subject and a score both imaginative and richly coloured. The designer skilfully solved the problem of historical costume with half-length overskirts and a silhouette suggesting farthingales for the female dancers, and a basic multi-purpose set adaptable for different locations, cued by

"Mary Queen of Scots"   (Anthony Crickmay)

"Othello"   (Jim Wilson)

a spotlit map of France, Scotland and England on a front-cloth.

Within this outline the ballet has some of Darrell's most classical choreography, both for the principal characters and in the expertly-handled ensemble scenes involving courtiers and commoners. His view of Mary as a woman of innate feminine charm, and of pleasure in the men in her life, is expressed through contrasted pas de deux, particularly with the febrile Darnley and the more sensual Bothwell. Imaginative choreographic distinctions are made between French and Scottish courtiers, and between the Scottish and English courts. In the first performances, besides Graham Bart's aggressively masculine Bothwell and the more willowy Darnley of Paul Tyers, there were outstanding individual performances from Kit Lethby's misshapen and virtuoso Riccio and Robin Haig's temperamental Elizabeth. The title role was originally shared between Elaine McDonald and Patricia Rianne, the former with a touchingly sorrowful sweetness of detail and the latter with a more passionate sweep of temperament. Both made the death scene hauntingly tragic.

It is possible that Darrell will make further revisions in a ballet so rich in choreographic and musical content as *Mary, Queen of Scots*. He was working towards another full-length ballet on the subject of Cinderella for the end of 1978, but this had to be postponed for budgetary reasons. When it comes about, instead of Prokofiev's ballet score for *Cinderella* (already used by Ashton for the Royal Ballet), Darrell's version will follow his *Hoffmann* model in having music adapted from Rossini's *La Cenerentola* (1817), which was, incidentally, the first musical representation of Cinderella on the English stage in 1820, and the operatic precursor of all the pantomime versions. Meanwhile, Darrell continued no less active. His trenchant *Othello* (1971), originally created for André Prokovsky's New London Ballet, was reproduced for the Ballet for Scotland tour repertory in 1976, and renewed its dramatic impact of fatal jealousy in terms of Shakespeare's characters, all within the scope and nature of the first

"Intimate Pages" (Anthony Crickmay)

79

movement from Liszt's *A Faust Symphony*. Darrell then made *Nightmare* (1976) for pub performances, and *Intaglio* (1977) as a further work for students. *Green Song* (also 1977) is a classical pas de deux for Patricia Merrin and Paul Tyers, and *Picnic* (1978) is a contribution to the Scottish Ballet Workshop's schools' programme, *Wowza!*

An echo of the captive but resigned Queen of Scots near the end of Darrell's ballet, combined with the expressive intensity of *O Caritas*, is found again in *Five Rückert Songs* (1978). 'A woman, disenchanted with the glamorous but passing pleasures of her life, finds within herself an inner peace' reads the programme rubric. The balletic character stems directly from the songs Mahler composed to poems of Friedrich Rückert, independent of each other but linked by feelings of withdrawal from the world, of intimate self-communion and a renewal of faith. There are ten dancers in support of the central role, which demands a true depth of expressive commitment, not least in the final song, which the woman dances alone. The role was divided between Eleanor Moore, Elaine McDonald and Sally Collard-Gentle in the performances given by separate groups in different locations during the Ballet for Scotland tour, and my own first impression of one of these suggested that this could well be a work for the company's main repertory as well.

Since then Darrell has reverted to the role of choreographic joker with his contribution to *Underground Rumours* (1979), a triple-bill of new ballets to jazz and popular music. Darrell's ballet took its title and its music from *Such Sweet Thunder*, a famous jazz suite composed by Duke Ellington and Billy Strayhorn and premiered in 1957, which takes a sidelong jazz view of a number of Shakespeare characters. Incorporating some of Ellington's own comments as a spoken sound-track (e.g. Lady Macbeth: 'We suspect she had a little ragtime in her soul'), Darrell carried the analogies a stage further and related each of Ellington's Shakespeareans to the showbiz celebrities of a more recent era. Ellington's 'Lady Mac' accordingly became Rita Hayworth, who was in turn Elaine McDonald in flaming red hair and black dress, emoting in all directions to create a wicked parody of both characters. Among the other double-identities (nearly thirty altogether) were Desdemona/Bette Davis (Gwendoline Edmonds); Titania/Marilyn Monroe (Sally Collard-Gentle); Oberon/Liberace (Paul Tyers); Othello/Sydney Poitier (Paul Russell) and Hamlet/Elvis Presley (Peter Mallek). Darrell risked a lot on his audience picking up the often subtle allusions of each. Although a few worked less well than others, the company put across their multiple portraits with imaginative panache in Bob Ringwood's designs, and Paul Hart's orchestral transcription of the Ellington music was skilfully done. The sharp eye and gift for parody, mixed with an unmistakable affection, that Darrell brought to his stage characters reveal an engaging side of his own character as well.

9.
From Far and Near

"Vespri"

(Jim Wilson)

Besides Peter Darrell's *Such Sweet Thunder*, the Scottish Ballet's first new programme of 1979 brought two ballets by other choreographers, Robert North (*The Water's Edge*) and Royston Maldoom (*Ursprung*). They add to an impressive tally of works by more than twenty choreographers of the present or recent past which have helped to extend the the company's main repertory. As already mentioned, the company's very first programme under its Scottish title comprised a nineteenth-century classic, *La Ventana*, and a new work, Gillian Lynne's *Breakaway*, which took the teenage scene of its time as a topic for comment and illustration, and which was also related to music in the idiom of the time, by Barry Booth. Since then, some of the works by 'outside' choreographers were already successes elsewhere before being newly produced for the Scottish repertory. Some were entirely new, and either came and went relatively quickly, or obtained a continuing interest and success over more than one season, as happened with Jack Carter's *Three Dances to Japanese Music* (1973).

Carter had previously worked for the company in its WTB days when he created *Cage of God* (1967), a dramatic morality which was one of his most original choreographic essays and which closely matched Darrell's preference for dramatic ballets involving few characters. It confirmed Carter's talent for sharply drawn dramatic character in dance which had been apparent since *The Witch Boy* (1956), on the American ballad of Barbara Allen.[1] After working for some time in Japan, Carter took the style of the Japanese Kabuki theatre as a starting-point for the first of the *Three Dances*, in which the River God steals a wife while her Lord is sleeping. The other two dances move progressively further away from Oriental models.

All three are set to authentic Japanese music which Carter collected in Japan, and which was recorded in arrangements for traditional instruments by Kisahisa Katada. Yet they are in no sense imitation folk-dances, but a free interpretation of ideas as seen through a Westerner's imagination, and enhanced by the elaborate Oriental

costumes and headdresses designed by Norman McDowell. In the second dance a woman enjoys the competitive attentions of two men while the family from the first dance look on, and the attenuated versions of Oriental costumes worn by the dancers here are continued in the third dance, which is virtually a plotless ensemble. Among the original cast there were memorable performances by a splendidly-masked Kit Lethby as the River God and Anna McCartney as the wife turned into a Kabuki ondine; by Marian St. Claire as the focus of the second dance, and by the five men who have some striking steps to begin the third. The music is the only real link between the dances, which are choreographically quite separate and different, but in performance they formed a satisfying trilogy which became very popular and was widely toured — to Australia, Paris and elsewhere.

Another Carter ballet a year later was *The Dancing Floor*, a version of the Minotaur legend in terms of Pasiphaë's lust for the White Bull. This had an existing all-electronic score by the American composer Morton Subotnick, itself called *The Wild Bull* and previously used by Glen Tetley for *Arena* (1969). It is often difficult to pinpoint precisely why one work succeeds where another does not, but in this instance Carter created an opening duet for Pasiphaë and Minos, danced initially by Marian St. Claire and Barry McGrath, bold in character as well as hectic in expression, which the rest of the work failed to sustain. The successive waves of dancing for a further trio of females, and an ensemble of five pairs, seemed too vaguely related to the ballet's ostensible theme, but it held a place in the repertory for several seasons to 1978.

Embers of Glencoe (1973) was the only entirely new work created for the company by the Scottish-born Walter Gore, a choreographer of experience and distinction — and the first Rake in Ninette de Valois' *The Rake's Progress* (1935). His light-hearted piece *Street Games* (1952) was a perennial favourite with Western Theatre Ballet and

---

[1] *The Witch Boy*, with music by Leonard Salzedo, was first created for the Ballet of the Lowlands in Holland and produced by London Festival Ballet in 1957, in whose repertory it remained for many years.

Cleo Nordi at a class   (Glasgow Herald)

was taken over with continuing popularity in the early days of the Scottish company, for whom he also mounted two other fun-ballets from the 1950s, *Peepshow* and *Light Fantastic*. It was not simply that *Glencoe* was a tragic subject whereas the others are comedy diversions, but the new ballet's character was diffused through a mixture of dance, speech, historical allusion and a percussion score, without the strength of choreographic invention to unite these diverse elements, so that it was one of Gore's few failures.

, Other choreographers of an older generation included Anton Dolin, who staged his *Pas de Quatre* (1941), derived from the famous Chalon lithograph of the four great nineteenth-century Romantic ballerinas,[2] and followed it with his *Variations for Four* (1957), a comparable divertissement for male dancers. Andrée Howard, who died in 1968, left her most vivid memorial in the poetic and sensitive *La Fête Etrange* (1940), which has reappeared from time to time in the Royal Ballet repertory, and which earned a deserved welcome in a production by the Scottish Ballet in 1971, with the choreography reproduced by Helen Starr.

It is derived from an episode in a French novel, Alain-Fournier's *Le Grand Meaulnes*, in which an adolescent's wondering innocence brings inevitable grief to himself and two adults, their feelings visible to the audience but not to each other. With an anthology of Fauré music, including two songs, *La Fête Etrange* has the faculty of suspending a moment in time with that poetic intensity which is one of the most haunting qualities of ballet. It benefited from the performances in the three principal roles of Elaine McDonald, Kenn Wells and Gordon Aitken in the first instance, and it restored the singer (Ann Baird) to a costumed stage presence instead of confining her to the orchestra pit, as happened in the Covent Garden performances. In its very restraint and subtlety it is a ballet well suited to the Scottish repertory, where I hope it will continue to be seen.

[2] Marie Taglioni, Carlotta Grisi, Fanny Cerrito, Lucile Grahn, who came together for a pas de quatre by Jules Perrot at Her Majesty's Theatre, London, in 1845.

"Pas de Quatre" (Anthony Crickmay)

Even older in origin but equally worth reviving is Antony Tudor's *Soirée Musicale* (1938), which had not been seen at all for many years before Tudor agreed to its production for the Ballet for Scotland tour in the Spring of 1973, stipulating that it should only be given on small stages. The ballet is the danced equivalent of a Victorian musical evening, in which the dancers entertain each other and their audience with a suite of gently contrasting character. It was staged from a Labanotation script by Ann Hutchinson, who also researched the original costume designs by Hugh Stevenson, most of which had long been sold to collectors, and the Rossini pieces which Benjamin Britten orchestrated were restored to their original piano form for touring purposes. Illness caused a last-minute juggling in roles, but Anne Allan in the bolero, Patricia Rianne with Harold King in the tirolese and Hilary Debden with Michael Beare in the tarantella were notably fine, and to have even light-weight work of such a choreographer in the repertory is better than having none.

The same tour programme brought the first of two ballets by André Prokovsky, both originally created for his own New London Ballet. *Scarlatti and Friends* (1972) was devised as an informal danced overture to introduce dancers in casual dress before a first main ballet, and the Scottish version was in fact the ballet's premiere in Britain (Glasgow, 17 January 1973), the New London Ballet at that time having performed only abroad. The second Prokovsky ballet, *Vespri* (1973), is a work on a larger scale and was mounted for the Ballet for Scotland repertory in October 1977, then expanded into a larger version with more dancers[3] at Glasgow the following March, and with a new setting by Norman McDowell suggesting the mirror-image of an audience in the theatre, which usually wins applause as soon as it is seen. It is a ballet of some grandeur in the classical style to the ballet suite from Verdi's opera, *Les Vêpres*

[3] The enlarged version of *Vespri*, with opening and closing ensembles for 16 male and 16 female dancers, and with a pas de quatre in place of a male solo, was previously performed only by the PACT Ballet in South Africa, for whom it was staged.

"Giselle" Act 1   (Anthony Crickmay)

Hazel Merry, Simon Mottram and Sylvia Wellman
in "Sonate à Trois"   (Anthony Crickmay)

Siciliennes, and provides an entertaining display of individual charm and brilliance. Patricia Merrin, with Graham Bart and Paul Russell; Linda Anning, Kenneth Burke and especially Vincent Hantam were able to take full advantage of its opportunities.

Some of the company's successful repertory ballets are by leading choreographers from abroad. The legacy of Western Theatre Ballet brought to Scotland an early work of Maurice Béjart in *Sonate à Trois* (1957), and also *The Lesson* (1963) by Flemming Flindt, his first work when he turned to choreography. Both suited the Darrell mould of sharply-chacterised dance-dramas for a small number of performers. Both had literary sources: Sartre for the sardonic suggestion in Béjart that 'Hell is other people'; Ionesco for Flindt's macabre murder-ploy (as a vehicle for character-study it was later taken up by Nureyev with much success). With music by Bartók and Georges Delerue respectively, each provided three roles of dramatic substance to extend the dancers — and new ideas about ballet to stretch their audiences.

Although no longer in the repertory, two later works created for the Scottish Ballet are worth recalling. *Frontier* (1969) was one of the first ballets by the American John Neumeier, now Director of Ballet at Hamburg. Classical in style and romantically expressive in character, it portrayed a simple boy-meets-girl encounter in a museum, where tapestries on display come to life in their imaginations, and made adept use of the Oboe Quintet by Sir Arthur Bliss. The poetic mood brought about by an everyday incident, by no means very original in its conception, reflected an inventive choreographic talent; it also resembled some aspects of *La Fête Etrange*, with which it shared the same leading dancers in McDonald and Wells.

An intriguing Dutch contribution was Toer van Schayk's *Ways of Saying Bye-bye* (1973), which acquired this title only after it was first performed at the Scottish Ballet's 'Fanfare for Europe' gala that year. Van Schayk, well known as a dancer and designer in the Dutch National Ballet from 1965, puzzled some people at first by the layers of abrupt contrasts in his ballet:

between elegance and primitiveness in the choreography; between heeled Baroque shoes and body-tights in the design; between Purcell and 'pop' in the music, and between misty illusion and harsh neon tubes in the lighting. It nevertheless brought about a new and entertaining development of style for the company, who danced it with evident relish, and audiences later warmed to it.[4]

Programmes of experimental and new work have consistently encouraged members of the company to develop any latent choreographic interest and talent, and the repertory has benefited by several works from them. Before he left to join the Royal Ballet in 1971, Ashley Killar created two works for experimental programmes, *Match for Three Players* and *Journey*. The first, involving a woman who creates an alter ego in the form of a female wrestler in an emotional tussle with a man, would have been taken into the main repertory if there had not been problems of musical copyright with the works concerned (by Mauricio Kagel and Olivier Messiaen). Instead, Killar was invited to make another ballet and produced *Arriving Bellevue Sunday* (1971). On a musical basis of three works by Janácek, the ballet portrayed the effect of a mysterious visitor on a decidedly unbalanced family (their origins were in Pasolini's film, *Theorem*). A style of movement basically expressionist in character offered the most enigmatic dancing to Kenn Wells and Brian Burn alternating as the stranger, and a meaty role as a murderously-inclined maidservant to Bronwen Curry and Dianne Richards.

The company's first ballet with a strong Gaelic flavour was *An Clò Mor* by its associate director, Stuart Hopps, first performed at the Citizens' Theatre, Glasgow, on 19 January 1972 and later toured widely including the Western Isles, which might be called its place of origin. It is a simple love-tale of a Lewis fisherman and his bride, and the 'big cloth' of the title is the tweed woven by the

---

4 Another work, *Moment* (1975), was created by the American Murray Louis for Nureyev and four other male dancers when the Scottish Ballet appeared at the Madrid dance festival, but it has not so far formed part of the regular repertory.

women which serves variously as a symbol of the sea, a ceremonial wrap or a shroud. The ballet stems from various Gaelic songs which were sung on stage by Dolina MacLennan, representing the *bean-turidh*, the 'knee-wife' who watches over comings and goings and weaves the fabric of Lewis life into song. In addition, a tape of Mary Morrison of Barra accompanied the ceremonial waulking of the cloth as the ballet's central focus, the primitive quality of voice and drums suggesting a timeless ritual.

Although Hopps himself had no Scottish connections, the ballet was widely acclaimed for its authenticity of spirit and character, the dancing being choreographed in a free style motivated by the songs which provided its essence. Patricia Rianne made much of the complex emotions expressed by the central female figure, with Stephen Lansley as the fisherman committed both to the sea and to his love. The choreographer was praised for having 'captured the spirit of an entirely alien culture and given it new life by setting it in a modern context'[5], and John Percival commented in *Dance and Dancers* (March

1972): 'It is a very simple piece, with something of the feeling of true folk art . . . even for a foreigner like myself the work has a genuine sense of life on the islands, a life in which pleasures are hard won, short-lived but truly enjoyed'.

Later the same year Hopps also made *Positively the Last Final Farewell Performance*, a sardonic anthology of victims of dramatic disappearances (such as Amelia Earhart, 'Buster' Crabbe, Colonel Fawcett, Leigh Mallory) whose destinies were portrayed with comic-strip vividness to the music of another disappearance-victim, Glenn Miller. Hopps described the work as 'a ballet without steps', but his inventive ideas produced some agreeably zany dancing. The same programme included *Some Bright Star* by Peter Cazalet, whose chief contribution, apart from dancing, was otherwise as the gifted designer of such productions as *Giselle*, *La Sylphide* and *Swan Lake*. However, *Some Bright Star* put eight dancers through their virtuoso paces in

---

[5] Gordon Gow, *Scottish International*, February 1972.

"Les Sylphides" with Elaine McDonald and Graham Bart   (Jim Wilson)

"An Clò Mor" with Steven Lansley and Patricia
Rianne   (Diane Tammes)

fluent, attractive choreography, and Elaine McDonald's sudden cry of distress as she succumbed to the strain of a long exposed solo concentrated for a moment, albeit deliberately, all the drama of what it takes to be a star dancer.

Another dancer, Harold King, turned his experimental *Homage à Rameau* into *Partie de Campagne* for the 1974 Ballet for Scotland repertory, and followed this the same year with *Intimate Pages*. This made a favourable impression as a ballet of no specific plot but strong emotional cross-currents, set to the equally eloquent music of Janácek's second String Quartet, itself titled 'Intimate Letters'.[6] A quirky solo for Kit Lethby showed the most inventive choreography, which was otherwise concerned mainly to express the intensity of emotional feeling brought about by the relationships suggested. Most recently Gordon Aitken was encouraged by *Autumn Song*, a modestly classic pas de deux he made for the 'Nework' programme in 1978, to create *Naila* for the Ballet for Scotland tour repertory the following year. An Oriental fantasy to music by Delibes (from *La Source*), it combines an exotic appeal of design by Bruno Santini with assured classical style.

A bridge between contemporary works and the 19th century has been furnished in two ballets from the early years of this century by the first great choreographer of Sergei Diaghilev's Russian Ballet, Mikhail Fokine. Western Theatre Ballet already had Fokine's *Le Carnaval* (1910) in its repertory, staged by Elisabeth Schooling, and this was remounted in 1973 for its first Scottish production. Bakst's costume designs were carefully reproduced by Elizabeth Dalton, and although the company lacked an ideal dancer for Harlequin at that time, there was warm praise for Gordon Aitken (Pierrot), Harry Haythorne (Pantalon), Anne Allan (Estrella), Marian St. Claire (alternately Columbine and Papillon), and an Australian newcomer, Dianne Storer, who shared Papillon with St. Claire.

Four years later Fokine's *Les Sylphides* (1909) was staged for the 1977 Edinburgh Festival performances with Natalia Makarova and Fernando Bujones as the

guest principals, and was later taken into the regular repertory for the first time at Glasgow the following March. The company's ballet mistress, Cecilia Barrett, skilfully taught the authentic choreography, and produced the ballet in an attractive Peter Cazalet setting of a tree-fringed glade. These performances were distinguished by Patricia Merrin's sustained line in the Prelude, Elaine McDonald's imposing Mazurka, and Andrea Durant, gossamer-light in the Waltz, with Peter Mallek firm but somewhat stiff as the male dancer.

Unlike other major companies in Britain, the Scottish Ballet has not sought any other reproductions from the Diaghilev era, and it was the experimental programme of 'Nework' early in 1979 which — beginning and ending as it did with two works to Stravinsky music by company members (Garry Trinder and William Bowen) — pointed the absence from the Scottish repertory of any Stravinsky ballets. This is a major gap in an otherwise wide range, and it may be hoped that future plans will take steps to fill it from the amazing variety of ballets to Stravinsky, whose music, more than that of any other composer, has changed and enriched the art of dance in this century.

---

[6] The same string quartet later became the basis of Lynn Seymour's *Intimate Letters* (1978) for the Sadler's Wells Royal Ballet.

10.
Touring

Veronica Butcher and Ruth Prior in their dressing
room   (William Cooper)

When The Scottish Ballet appears in any one of the thirty to forty towns and cities now regularly visited in the course of a year's work, its performance will be the outcome of a complex scheme of planning and organisation which may have begun up to two years before. This is the length of time ahead when preliminary decisions are taken by Peter Darrell and Robin Anderson about the kind of repertory they would like to see available 'the year after next': what new works might be in prospect, and what others can be revived. Such plans, of course, may need to undergo several changes before the repertory is confirmed, and all planning has to be an act of faith when the amount of public funds from the Scottish Arts Council and other sources is only on a year-to-year basis, and is never known until after commitments have to be made. This chapter explores the process by which the company reaches its audiences, and the way in which the Scottish Ballet Workshop complements it.

The broad structure of a year's work now defines itself on the basis of past experience. So far as the main company is concerned it will usually consist of a Spring tour from about March until May; a Summer season at Edinburgh and Glasgow if sufficient funds are available, and/or an occasional foreign visit; a Ballet for Scotland tour in the Autumn, for which the company is divided into two smaller ensembles, each touring the same repertory, and a Christmas season based on Aberdeen, Edinburgh and Glasgow in turn. Between each of these major activities, a rehearsal period of at least three to five weeks is needed to prepare the repertory, when the dancers continue to work long hours in the studio getting the next batch of performances together. Even the revival of two existing ballets may need four weeks of rehearsal to bring them up to standard, and a new ballet will take correspondingly longer to make ready.

With the outline of work in mind, and the possible repertory planned, the places to be visited are next considered. This is done on the basis of direct contact between the administrator and the theatres concerned, who first of all suggest particular weeks or dates they would like the ballet to appear. So far as possible, a tour is planned to minimise the tiring effect of travel, and one theatre may be asked to exchange weeks with another elsewhere until a pattern emerges, but some awkward journeys for the dancers and staff may become unavoidable. Any vacant weeks left over from requirements in Scotland may be offered to the Touring Department of the Arts Council of Great Britain in London to fill with dates in England. In any case the result is always the best possible compromise between what the company would like to do, and what it is able to do in practical and economic terms when the ordinary costs of the company are £10,500 a week and the additional costs of touring amount to £18,000 to £20,000 a week more.

Having decided where and when the company will appear some twelve months ahead, it then becomes time to have a technical discussion about the intended repertory for each place. This involves Peter Searle as technical director, with the master carpenter, Peter Thorpe, and the chief electrician, Ian Irving, and also the wardrobe supervisor, Caro Harkness. They will advise on what is technically practicable for the theatres concerned, how the scenery will fit and the lighting relate, whether the changeovers from one programme to another are feasible, and how much renovation of costumes and decor a particular ballet may require. Even to revive a relatively straightforward work like André Prokovsky's *Vespri* after some years will take perhaps £2,000 for new costumes, and it may be that plans will still have to be changed because the costs of renovating a particular ballet cannot be afforded within the budget at that time.

Where a new ballet involves costumes being made to a designer's sketches, the designer will need to book time with the costume-makers at least nine months ahead. He or she will give advice on who can best execute the designs, and will oversee the actual making-up of them. As an average rule-of-thumb figure, each costume will cost about £200 for materials and the making. They could be made more cheaply, but they would then wear out much sooner and require replacement. In order to look good on stage costumes have to withstand constant wear and tear in performance and being moved about, as well as regular cleaning and

storage. After the Glasgow headquarters are fully operating, the company hopes that more wardrobe work can be undertaken there, but they will never be able to make all their own costumes.

Technical as well as musical considerations also involve the music director, Bramwell Tovey, and the orchestra manager, Clive Thomas. They will need to know and advise on the facilities each theatre has for accommodating an orchestra, as well as any problems connected with the music as such. It will be little use, for instance, to programme a ballet which depends on an orchestra of forty-five if the theatre concerned can find room to seat only twenty-five players. Once the musical requirements are met, the music director will plan what rehearsal time he will need for the works to be performed, once the orchestra has come together. The orchestra manager does not begin to book individual players, however, until about three months before the tour, when there is more chance of engaging better musicians who may be reluctant to commit themselves any earlier. On present work-schedules the company can offer orchestra players full employment for probably twenty weeks a year, and thereby hope to attract perhaps a higher standard of musician than if they were seeking players for fifty weeks of pit work.

Most theatres visited by the company are well enough known by now in terms of their special problems or advantages, but if a new theatre is involved a technical investigation will have to be made on the spot about three months ahead to find out what its exact facilities or snags are. Even with a familiar theatre today, stage staffs will often be quite different from one visit to the next, and so time has to be allowed for showing them everything a production needs to work smoothly. Lighting and setting consequently take more time, and the usual practice on weekly visits now is to get in the productions on a Sunday night, light them overnight, have technical rehearsals on Monday and a 'placing' call for the dancers that evening, and open the performances on a Tuesday.

The relations and practical arrangements with each theatre is the responsibility of the general manager, Roger Spence. He will

Preparing the Costumes for "Underground Rumours" (William Cooper)

negotiate the theatre charges and ticket prices, what concessionary schemes might be offered, whether a midweek matinée can be given. He will also supervise the promotions and publicity work of Veronica Colin as marketing officer and Geoffrey Baskerville as Press officer, in the links that can be set up with local television, radio, newspapers and other outlets to promote the company's visit. These arrangements will probably be made about two months ahead, when it is also decided if a visit by Jim Hastie and his introductory programme, 'Prelude to the Ballet', is desirable in advance of the company, and what will be done about pictures, posters and other 'front of house' publicity.

The general manager must also make arrangements for transporting the dancers and scenery from one theatre to another. The scenery, props and costumes travel in three or four trucks, hired from specialists who have developed their service in response to the specific needs of touring the Scottish Ballet and Scottish Opera. Usually the vehicles are returned as soon as a get-in to a theatre has

been made, to wait until required for the next weekend's move, but in some places the theatre may not be able to provide storage for scenery, and a trailer may then have to be kept in attendance throughout the week to act as a scenery-dock.

The dancers are taken from one centre to another by coach, again rented for each journey, but nowadays usually the same coach with a special sign proclaiming the company name. On the major tours the dancers find their own accommodation in each place they visit, paying for it from a special touring allowance negotiated for them with British Actors' Equity on the reasonable basis that dancers should be able to afford modest hotel accommodation, if they wish, like other people who travel regularly for business. By agreement with the Musicians' Union, a similar provision is made for the orchestra, but the players make their own travel arrangements. On the Ballet for Scotland tours the accommodation is booked in advance, because of the complex network of one, two or three-night visits criss-crossing Scotland and covering as much as 5,000

Scottish Ballet Workshop in "Wowza!"
(William Cooper)

"UFO Show"

miles by the two groups on one tour.

All the problems are magnified on tours abroad. For Australia and New Zealand in 1974 the scenery, props and costumes had to be sent by sea, which meant that the productions concerned could not be available for any other performances in the six to eight weeks both before and after the tour. Even a short visit to Spain, like that in 1978, may require the necessary production materials to be sent out direct from midweek performances at home to be at the destination in time. So the next time you see the curtain go up on a Scottish Ballet performance, spare a thought for the thousand and one details that had to be brought together at the right time and in the right place for it to happen at all. The staff themselves will have no such thoughts to spare: they will already be concerning themselves with next week, the week after that — or even what may, will or should be happing this time next year.

*   *   *

Different factors govern the nature and operation of the Scottish Ballet Workshop, which Sue Weston has developed into a vital supplementary aspect of the company's work in Scotland. She and the five dancers, with pianist, manager and technician, devote much of their effort to work in schools, bringing dance performances of a professional standard to schoolchildren of various ages, encouraging their interest in dance by demonstrating the dancer's craft, and actively involving many of them in creative sessions where they learn to move and invent dance for themselves. The Workshop also gives demonstrations and performances for adult audiences in such locations as community centres, and will tour a full programme of ballet to remote areas where the main company could never appear, like the northern and western islands.

To carry out such a varied pattern of work requires, in the first place, dancers of a particular commitment who must be something of an élite in the versatile qualities they are called on to display. Sue Weston does not believe that they need to be too concerned about relating to children: she insists that a combination of intelligent common sense and a high level of technique are the fundamental

requirements. The dancing must always come first; a relationship to children will follow from the ability to dance well for them. Individual roles for each dancer can change about from day to day, and from one school to the next, so that they have to give constant thought to what they are doing and the way in which it fits into the programme as a whole.

During its most recent season (1978-79) the Workshop toured a notably successful schools programme devised by Sue Weston under the title of *Wowza!* It explores as an entertainment the various relationships between dance and sport, in bodily rhythms and muscular movements, and in the similarities or contrasts of technique and discipline. The programme first took shape in the director's mind some nine months before it came to performance. She began actively to prepare it about six months ahead, then lost the composer and designer who were to be involved, which meant that she started afresh with something different again, related to the basic theme, and the content and character of the programme was constantly modified as it came together in detail.

Like the main company, the Workshop has evolved a general pattern of annual activity. It is centred on a grant from Strathclyde Regional Council for nine weeks work in the region, usually two weeks in the Autumn and the rest spread through the Winter when, for practical reasons, the group stays close to its Glasgow base, and its dancers can supplement the main company for the major Christmas productions. Four weeks in the late Spring or Summer are given to touring Orkney, Shetland and the Western Isles, and there are usually engagements of a week or more on offer from Tayside, Fife and Grampian. Lothian and Central have yet to support their work, and for the Highland region they have so far been engaged by the Highland and Islands Development Board in the absence of funds from the regional authority.

Arrangements are made by post or telephone direct with the schools and other places to be visited, and these are reached by minibus. Because of the amount of travelling involved between one-day or one-night stands — sometimes a school performance in the afternoon and an adult programme in the evening — bookings are made on the basis of a five-day week, with occasional weeks of not more than three or four working days so that the members of the Workshop can get back to Glasgow or have a long weekend free of performances and travel. An additional strain is imposed on the Workshop dancers by the closer contact with their audiences, compared with theatre conditions, in which they generally find themselves performing.

Moreover, the Workshop seldom finds itself appearing in theatrical conditions. More often than not it is a school hall or gymnasium, with or without a stage at one end, but bare of all except functional necessities. The programme will have been evolved so that it can technically be fitted into most spaces, but the Workshop likes to give its audiences the illusion of theatre, 'to go into a room and make it look good', as Sue Weston puts it, and they have developed to a high degree this ability to make theatrical magic in unlikely circumstances. Indeed, some of their audiences have been attracted in the first place by watching the technical preparations — the laying of a Marley floor (on which the dancers first of all take a regular daily class wherever they are), setting lights and so on — which then leads them to take an interest in the outcome in performance.

The Workshop's function in schools is seen by its director as complementing the work of existing teachers, not replacing them in any way at all. But to this end she plans to develop, if possible, more support for teachers and to provide in-service courses for them to extend their knowledge and practice of dance, so that they can continue with their pupils where the Workshop has to leave off in order to move on to the next place to be visited. Having begun almost entirely with girls, the group is finding that more and more boys are becoming involved, especially when school staffs discover (often to their surprise) that the members of the Workshop are just as efficient in capturing and controlling the interest of boys as they are with girls. Opportunities are also taken to encourage and give practical advice or assistance to amateur dancers and dance groups wherever these are found.

Indeed, the Scottish Ballet Workshop is very much a service to the community as a

Gordon Aitken taking class   (Bob Anderson)

whole; the increasing numbers who attend its performances (and the places where it is welcomed back) testify to the success it has already had. Sue Weston's declared intention is to bring to as wide an area as possible a cameo of professional performance in a manner that will give dignity to the work of the dancers she directs, and the nature of the programmes they perform. Having brought about a demand for their work, it would be sad if the economic constraints threatening all the performing arts forced not merely a standstill on expansion, but an actual cut-back in what can be done. By the nature of its activity, the Scottish Ballet Workshop is a form of valuable investment in the future of The Scottish Ballet as a whole, to which our final chapter must now turn.

Susan Cooper in "Sofa Sleeves" for Scottish Ballet Workshop (William Cooper)

11.
The Next Steps

Cecilia Barrett coaches the company
(William Cooper)

All that has happened in the Scottish Ballet's first ten years augurs strongly for a continued development along the lines it has already firmly drawn. From discussion with members of Scottish Ballet's staff it appears that not many major changes are in prospect for the company as a whole. It is unlikely, for instance, that the company will expand much further in size from the basis of the forty-six dancers who now make up its main strength. This is the minimum number with which Peter Darrell, as artistic director, and the management and Board of Directors supporting him, consider it possible to produce and perform adequately the major classics in the repertory. Nevertheless, if and when funds allowed, a few more dancers would be welcomed as insurance against illness or injury. Especially on long tours, this would help to relieve the strain of ensuring that all the roles are adequately covered.

There would in any case be little sense in trying to make the company bigger in the economic conditions prevailing at the time this is written, when worldwide inflation often cuts the value of money, year by year, faster than funds can be obtained to compensate for it. At its present size the Scottish Ballet not only does well by its own audiences, in relation to the theatres available in Scotland, but it is also more attractive for touring elsewhere, in England and further afield, where the present-day costs of travel, accommodation and subsistence make it difficult, and sometimes impossible, to tour larger companies in the way they once were, unless a vast amount of extra public money is made available.

At the same time, there are ways in which a company can and should develop which have nothing to do with size. As this account has shown, there has always been a policy of encouraging choreographic talent among members of the Scottish company, for instance, when occasions have allowed. The new headquarters premises at 261 West Princes Street now make it possible to have more frequent and more informal experimental evenings than the once-a-year programmes hitherto given, with the possibility that the more successful works tried out in a small studio theatre can then be given in a medium-scale theatre later. A reasonable turnover of new works is essential for the interests of the company and its audiences, not to mention the health of ballet in general.

In this respect it is a reassurance to know that Darrell intends to maintain the wide range of repertory and styles for which the company has become well-known and widely admired, a policy that comprises new versions of established classics and new ballets relevant to the present time. Such a mixture has proved as beneficial to the company as it is stimulating to their audiences, who have had the opportunity to discover, for example, the reasons why the Bournonville ballets have become classics, with virtues of their own that are worth preserving and performing for modern audiences. The dancers, in turn, have acquired a versatility which is matched by few other companies, and which finds them as much at home in Bournonville and other nineteenth-century classics as in Robert North and other contemporary choreographers.

Some of this versatility is the fruit of extra cultivation by an increased ballet staff, particularly in the last two years when Gordon Aitken has been joined by Cecilia Barrett, Sue Carlton-Jones, Tony Hulbert and Diana Curry. Each is now able to give closer attention to various aspects of the dancers' continuing training, and the coaching of different styles and roles among individual dancers. The technique each dancer possesses at the time of joining the company accordingly becomes a springboard to other qualities in professional performances. Distinguished guest teachers engaged for short periods to give master-classes also help the company to acquire an added distinction of character and personality. Dancers of today have become steadily more skilled as the demands on them have become more severe.

This has brought into clearer focus the need for more extensive training for dance within Scotland, to develop it as a desirable skill in more children of both sexes, and to give those that want to make it their career the best kind of vocational training, whether it be for classical ballet or for other forms of dancing in the different outlets the profession provides. The weekly scholarship classes run by the Scottish Ballet have been invaluable as far as they could go, and have already brought five dancers into the company (and a sixth with Scottish Opera),[1] but the next step in prospect is the setting up of a wider scheme of dance education which will eventually provide a comparable level of training to that of the Royal Ballet School in London.

The initiative for this was taken in 1978 when the Scottish Ballet's Board of Directors authorised the formation of a working party to examine the possibilities and recommend a plan. Under the chairmanship of Robin Anderson, the working party has consisted of Peter Darrell, Gordon Aitken and Cecilia Barrett from the Scottish Ballet; Veronica Bruce (representing the North of Scotland); Barbara Fewster (the Royal Ballet School); John Field (Royal Academy of Dancing); Ivy Kerr (Strathclyde Education Department); Lilian MacNeil (West of Scotland); Nancy Moore (Scottish Dance Teachers' Alliance); Jack Spurgeon (East of Scotland) and Peggy Woodeson (Dunfermline College of Further Education), with an observer from the Scottish Education Department. Comments were invited from teachers, parents or other interested persons.

A report in preparation is expected to recommend a three-tier regional scheme, at first covering mainly the central area of Scotland, but expanding into the more northerly areas within two years. At the primary level, children from the ages of eight to eleven would be provided with two dance classes a week, outside school hours and on a fee-paying basis, arrangements being made to fund scholarships for children whose parents could not otherwise afford the fees. Talented children at the secondary level will have a daily dance class within the school timetable, attending a properly equipped studio maintained by a selected secondary school, for which arrangements are already in hand with the Lothian and Strathclyde Regional authorities.

The teaching staff for these secondary classes will be provided and maintained by the Scottish Ballet, and the children chosen to attend them will be funded entirely through the state education scheme without further payment. Once the pupil has passed the

[1] Eleanor More; Kenneth Burke; Louise Hellewell; Elizabeth Peden; Pauline Laverty; Elaine Bryce is with Scottish Opera.

Gordon Aitken, Robert North, Ian Anderson and Robin Anderson during rehearsals of "The Water's Edge" (Peter Roy Watson)

NAPOLI ACT I
Young Girl (Flirt)

thin voile blouse
lace edged
decorated
high bodice
false lacing

striped skirt
over
net
understirts

white appliquéd
apron

Peter Cazalet's design for The Flirt in "Napoli"
(Bryan & Shear) 102

school-leaving age, and intends to make a career in dance, arrangements will be made for a further two years of intensive vocational training at the Scottish Ballet's headquarters. The financing of this stage has yet to be settled, but at the time of writing it is hoped that this will be done through local authority further education schemes, privately sponsored scholarships, or a combination of both. At the top of this third tier it is intended that the successful student will be fully trained for a career in dance, whether with the Scottish Ballet or other professional dance companies in Britain and abroad, or in other outlets for the dancer in the theatre and television.

When this can be brought about, the future of dance as an art and an entertainment will become that much more assured by the flow of properly trained new talent year by year. At the same time the encouragement of an interest in dance among a wider range of children, most of whom will never become dancers themselves, cannot but benefit the dance scene in general. As audiences for the present and future grow up knowledgeable as well as interested, they thereby help to raise the level of dance artistry all round. In an essay, 'What makes a dancer's life' in *Step by Step* (W.H. Allen, 1977), Dame Ninette de Valois wrote: 'Ballet is first of all concerned with the conception of what can be obtained through the development of a perfect body — or one as near perfection as Nature will allow . . . intelligence, musicality and character all play a sensitive yet positive part . . . and if you discipline movement in this way you help to discipline your attitude to life'.

The art of dance has taught us to discover that movement is all around us and within us; that disciplined movement is a means to both physical and mental well-being, and that the poetry of movement for an artistic purpose is its highest and most rewarding form of expression. It is a stimulation to the mind and a satisfaction to the senses paralleled only by music in its range and variety. Dancing for its own sake is an instinct for communication as old as mankind, but it is a measure of the Scottish

"The Water's Edge" (Peter Roy Watson)

Ballet's achievement in its first ten years to have shown to many thousands — as it will to many thousands more — how the poetic rhythm of bodily movement is as much a source of beauty as the span of melody, the form of a pictorial image, or the flow of words in our infinitely precious store of human happiness.

"Soirée Musicale"   (Anthony Crickmay)

Appendices

Andrea Durant and Nigel Spencer in "Belong"
(Jim Wilson)

The new headquarters at 261 West Princes Street,
Glasgow were occupied on 3rd July 1978, although
the building was not finally complete until the end of

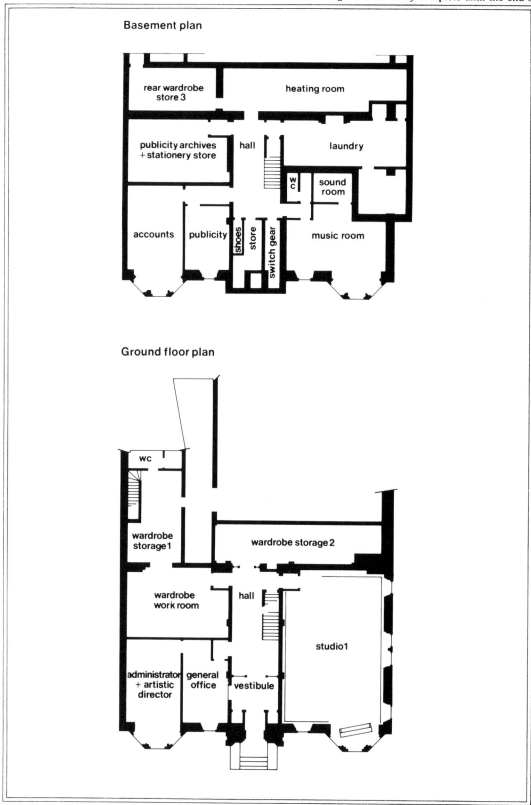

Basement plan

Ground floor plan

October. Plans were prepared by William T. Davie for conversion of the former Territorial Army Reserve Drill Hall.

First floor plan

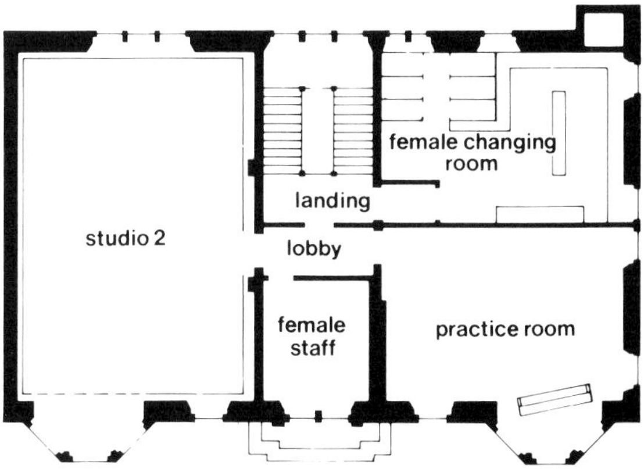
female changing room
landing
studio 2
lobby
female staff
practice room

Second floor plan

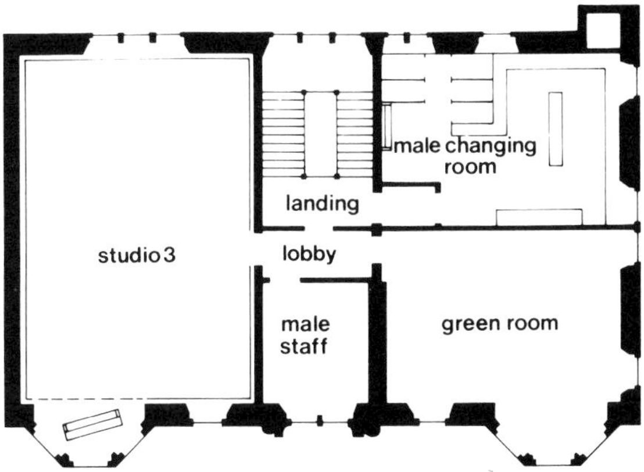
male changing room
landing
studio 3
lobby
male staff
green room

Third floor plan

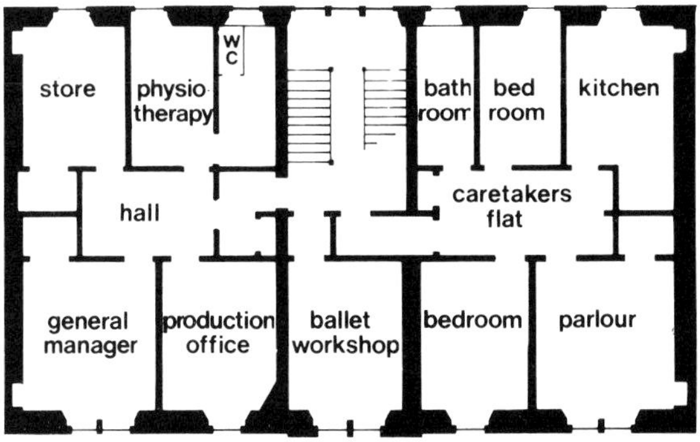
WC
store
physio therapy
bath room
bed room
kitchen
hall
caretakers flat
general manager
production office
ballet workshop
bedroom
parlour

THE SCOTTISH BALLET
STATISTICAL TABLE
1969-1978

Legend:
- OPERATING SURPLUS/DEFICIT AS % OF TOTAL EXPENDITURE
- EARNED INCOME AS % OF TOTAL INCOME
- TOTAL NO. OF SEATS SOLD (1977–8 = 100)

%: 10, 20, 30, 40, 50

Year	Operating surplus/deficit	Earned income	Seats sold	Overseas tours
1969-70	−£398	£7,497	NOT AVAILABLE	
1970-71	−£624	£18,790	26,130	
1971-72	−£2,764	£35,895	61,771	
1972-73	−£13,015	£45,162	56,111	
1973-74	£1,345	£55,785	65,876	
1974-75	£16,681	£102,816	67,045	(Australasian) + 132,029
1975-76	£6,591	£191,637	107,078	(Spain) + 27,695
1976-77	£12,371	£220,038	137,524	(Paris) + 34,483
1977-78	£49,958	£206,117	140,974	

ADDITIONAL AUDIENCE FOR OVERSEAS TOURS

%: 10, 20, 30, 40, 50, 60, 70, 80, 90

CHRONOLOGY OF PRODUCTIONS
(Dates in brackets record first performances)

1969/70 SEASON

Beauty and the Beast
(New production — 19 November 1969, Sadler's Wells Theatre, London. First performance in Scotland 9 December 1969, King's Theatre, Edinburgh)

Music	Thea Musgrave
	(commissioned score, with grant from
	Gulbenkian Foundation)
Choreography	Peter Darrell
Scenario and Production	Colin Graham
Design	Peter Minshall

Breakaway
(New production — 25 May 1969, King's Theatre, Glasgow)

Music	Barry Booth
	(commissioned score)
Choreography	Gillian Lynne
Design	Peter Cazalet

Cage of God
Music	Alan Rawsthorne
Choreography	Jack Carter
Design	Patrick Procktor

Ephemeron
Music	Milhaud
Choreography	Peter Darrell
Design	Peter Docherty

Frontier
(New production — 30 October 1969, Perth Theatre)

Music	Arthur Bliss
Choreography & Design	John Neumeier

The Lesson
Music	Georges Delerue
Choreography	Flemming Flindt
Design	Bernard Daydé

Spectrum
Music	Malcolm Williamson
Choreography	Clover Roope
Design	Charles Dunlop

La Ventana
Music	Lumbye
Choreography	Bournonville
Design	John Stoddart

The Trojans
(Joint production with Scottish Opera — 3 May 1969, King's Theatre, Glasgow)

Music	Berlioz
Choreography	Laverne Meyer
Production	Peter Ebert
Design	Hans Ulrich Schmuckle &
	Sylta Busse Schmuckle

Ballet at the Close
(Third choreographic workshop — 21 January 1970, Close Theatre Club, Glasgow)
The programme consisted of works by the following members of Company: —

Brian Burn	(to music by Mick Jagger,
	Keith Richards and Bill Wyman)
Ashley Killar	(to music by Mauricio Kagel)
Gernot Petzold	(to music by William Kraft)
Domy Reiter	(to music by J.S. Bach)
Tatsuo Sakai	(to traditional Japanese Music)
Kenn Wells	(to music by Villa-Lobos)

(A long extract from Ashley Killar's ballet **Match for Three Players** was later shown on BBC television in Scotland).

NEW PRODUCTIONS 1970/71

Large Scale Tour

Points of Contact
(13 July 1970, Sadler's Wells Theatre, London)

Music	Bob Woolford
	(electronic tape)
Choreography	Clover Roope
Design	Stephen Simmonds

Dances from William Tell
(13 July 1970, Sadler's Wells Theatre, London)

Music	Rossini
Choreography	Bournonville
	(reproduced by Hans Brenaa)
Design	Alix Stone

Herodias
(13 July 1970, Sadler's Wells Theatre, London)

Music	Hindemith
Choreography	Peter Darrell
Design	Peter Docherty
Production Consultant	Vincent Guy)

Giselle
(30 March 1971, His Majesty's Theatre, Aberdeen)

Music	Adam
	(arr. Humphrey Searle)
Choreography	Corelli & Perrot
	(reproduced by Joyce Graeme)
Design	Peter Cazalet
Production	Peter Darrell

Ploys Programme

Landscape
(9 September 1970, The Place, London)
Music   Brian Hodgson
                                         (electronic tape)
Choreography & Design   Peter Logan
                                         and Karl Brown
Consultant Engineer   Mike Reardon

Lovedu
(9 September 1970, The Place, London)
Music   Leonard Salzedo
Choreography   Kenn Wells
Design   Robin Cameron Don

Whirlpool
(9 September 1970, The Place, London)
Music   Takemitsu
Choreography & Design   Peter Cazalet

Sleepers
(9 September 1970, The Place, London)
Choreography   Stuart Hopps
Design   Charles Dunlop

Maze
(9 September 1970, The Place, London)
Music   Debussy, Matsudaira & Varese
Choreography & Design   Gernot Petzold

Journey
(25 September 1970, George Square Theatre,
Edinburgh)
Music   Janácek
Choreography   Ashley Killar

Scottish Arts Council Tour

Four Portraits
(1 February 1971, McLaren High School,
Callander)
Music   Prokofiev
Choreography   Peter Darrell
Design   Peter Docherty

Peepshow
(1 February 1971, McLaren High School,
Callander)
Music   Jean Francaix
Choreography & Design   Walter Gore

MAIN TOUR REPERTOIRE 1971/72

Giselle

Beauty and the Beast

La Fête Etrange
(14 October 1971, King's Theatre, Edinburgh)
Music   Fauré
Choreography   Andrée Howard
                              (reproduced by Helen Starr)
Scenario   Ronald Crichton
    (suggested by an episode in Alain-Fournier's
                           novel Le Grand Meaulnes)
Design   Sophie Fedorovitch

Arriving Bellevue Sunday
(14 October 1971, King's Theatre, Edinburgh)
Music   Janácek
Choreography   Ashley Killar
Design   Margaret Mary Preece

La Ventana

Performances given in:
Glasgow   Stirling
Edinburgh   Liverpool
Aberdeen   Billingham
Perth   Oxford
Swansea   Wolverhampton
Blackpool   Norwich
Sunderland
Manchester   Zurich
                           (two performances)

**Choreographic Workshop (26 January 1972,
Notre Dame College, Glasgow)**

Iseult
Music   Boris Blacher
Choreography   Gernot Petzold*

Transfigured
Music   Schoenberg
Choreography   Nicholas Carroll*

* Both these choreographers were dancers with the
company at the time of this workshop.

BALLET FOR SCOTLAND TOUR:
JANUARY-FEBRUARY 1972

Dances from William Tell

Journey

An Clò Mor (The Big Cloth)
(19 January 1972, Citizens' Theatre, Glasgow)
Music   Traditional
Choreography   Stuart Hopps
Scenario in collaboration with   George Reid
Costumes   Audrie Gie

"Home" with Suzanne Hywel, Robin Haig, Peter
Cazalet   (Anthony Crickmay)

111

Street Games
(New production — 4 April 1972, King's Theatre, Edinburgh)

Music   Ibert
Choreography   Walter Gore
Design   André Francois

COMPANY TOUR REPERTOIRE:
APRIL-MAY 1972

Tales of Hoffmann
(6 April 1972, King's Theatre, Edinburgh)

Music   Offenbach
                          (arranged John Lanchbery)
Choreography   Peter Darrell
Design   Alistair Livingstone
Lighting   John B. Read

The Lesson

La Fête Etrange

Street Games

Performances given in:
Edinburgh   Hull
Glasgow   Cardiff
Aberdeen

Ochtertyre Festival, Crieff (16-17 June 1972)

An Clò Mor

Tales of Hoffman (Pas de trois — Prologue)

Giselle (Pas de deux — Act II)

The Nutcracker (Pas de deux — Act II)

La Ventana (Pas de trois)

Street Games

Tangents
(28 June 1972, Close Theatre, Glasgow)

Variations for a Door and a Sigh
Music   Pierre Henry
Choreography   Peter Darrell
Design   Amanda Colin

Some Bright Star
Choreography & Design   Peter Cazalet
Music   Pink Floyd/Ivo Malec/
                          Tonto's Expanding Headband

Balkan Sobranie
Choreography   Richard Alston
Music   Stravinsky/Francaix/Fukushimo
Design   Myra Visser

Postively the Last Final Farewell Performance
Choreography   Stuart Hopps
Music   Glenn Miller Favourites
Design   Alan Alexander

Performances given in:
Glasgow
Edinburgh (Festival Fringe)

Choreographic Workshop (1-2 June 1972)

Rachmaninov Pas de Six
Music   Rachmaninov
Choreography   James Supervia

Scope
Music   Scriabin
Choreography   Gernot Petzold

Vivaldi + 4
Music   Vivaldi
Choreography   Brian Burn

Interval
Music   Bob Downes
Choreography   Cecilia Macfarlane

The Hollow Mask
Music   Bartok; Emerson, Lake & Palmer
Choreography   Stephen Lansley

Good 'Ol Sambo
Music   Gershwin
Choreography   Anthony West

Reverence to Rameau
Music   Rameau
Choreography   Harold King

Ploys (25-27 September 1972)

Landscape

Match for 3 Players
Music   Mauricio Kagel
Choreography   Ashley Killar

Lovedu (The People of the Rain Queen)

Whirlpool

Sleepers

Maze

Performances given in:
London   Glasgow
Edinburgh   Newcastle

AUTUMN TOUR REPERTOIRE:
OCTOBER 1972

Tales of Hoffmann

Light Fantastic
Music   Emmanuel Chabrier
Choreography   Walter Gore
(reproduced by Harry Haythorne)
Design   Jack Notman

Cage of God

Sonata à Trois
Music   Bartok
Choreography   Maurice Béjart
Decor   Adrian Vaux
Costumes   Peter Cazalet

Nutcracker (Act II)
Music   Tchaikovsky
Orchestrated by   Leonard Salzedo
Choreography   Lev Ivanov/Peter Darrell
Design   Philip Prowse

Performances given in:
Newcastle   Edinburgh
Billingham   Glasgow
Aberdeen   Stirling

GALA PERFORMANCE
(January 1973, King's Theatre Glasgow)

Street Games

Fanfare for Europe 1973

La Ventana

Flower Festival at Genzano (Pas de deux)

Valse Excentrique

Scorpius (Premiere)

Nutcracker (Pas de deux)

Tango Chikane

BALLET FOR SCOTLAND TOUR:
JANUARY-FEBRUARY 1973

Scarlatti and Friends
Music   Alessandro Scarlatti,
Domenico Scarlatti & Nicolai Fiorenza
Choreography   André Prokovsky

Beauty and the Beast
Music   Ravel
Choreography   John Cranko
Design   Peter Farmer

An Clò Mor

Flower Festival at Genzano (Pas de deux)
Music   Helsted & Paulli
Choreography   Auguste Bournonville

Some Bright Star

Peepshow
Music   Jean Francaix
Choreography   Walter Gore (for LJHB)

Nutcracker (Pas de deux)

Soirée Musicale
Music   Rossini
Choreography   Antony Tudor
Design   after Hugh Stevenson

Performances given in:
Dundee   Aberdour
Prestwick   Kilmarnock
Airdrie   Dumfries
Greenock   Strathaven
Duns   Beith
Prestonpans   Troon
Anstruther   Kirkcudbright

SPRING TOUR: MARCH-MAY 1973

Giselle

Nutcracker (Act II)

Ways of Saying Bye Bye
(7 January 1973)
Music   Purcell/Poptie/Pickett/
Harbach/Hoschna
Choreography & Design   Toer van Schayk

Le Carnaval
Music   Schumann
Choreography   Mikhail Fokine
Design   after Leon Bakst

Performances given in:
Bradford   Cardiff
Edinburgh   Swansea
Glasgow   Aberdeen
Birmingham

Marian St. Claire in "The Dancing Floor"
(Anthony Crickmay)

BALLET AT THE GATEWAY: AUGUST 1973
STV Studios, Edinburgh

Soirée Musicale

Sonate à Trois

Jeux
Music	Debussy
Choreography	Peter Darrell
Costumes	Harry Waistnage

Scorpius
Music	Thea Musgrave
Choreography	Peter Darrell

Valse Excentrique
Music	Ibert
Choreography	Kenneth MacMillan
Costumes	Lesley Bull

Three Dances to Japanese Music (premiere)
(20 August 1973)
Music	Traditional
	(arranged by Kisahisa Katada)
Choreography	Jack Carter
Costumes	Norman McDowell

AUTUMN TOUR:
OCTOBER-NOVEMBER 1973

Ways of Saying Bye Bye

La Sylphide
(25 September 1973, Theatre Royal, Nottingham)
Music	Herman von Lovenskjold
	(arranged by Allan Morgan)
Choreography	Auguste Bournoville
	(reproduced by Hans Brenaa)
Scenario	Adolphe Nourrit
Design	Peter Cazalet
Lighting	Molly Friedel

Embers of Glencoe (Premiere)
Music for percussion	Thomas Wilson
Choreography	Walter Gore
Design	George Devlin

Ephemeron

Flower Festival at Genzano (pas de deux)

Three Dances to Japanese Music

Performances given in:
Nottingham	Edinburgh
Glasgow	Bradford
Stirling	Sunderland
Aberdeen	Billingham

CHRISTMAS SEASON:
DECEMBER-JANUARY 1973-74
Royal Lyceum Theatre, Edinburgh

The Nutcracker
(19 December 1973)

AUSTRALASIAN TOUR
25 MARCH - 11 MAY, 1974
(with Margot Fonteyn and Ivan Nagy)

La Sylphide

Three Dances to Japanese Music

The Nutcracker (Act II)

La Ventana

Sonata à Trois

Tales of Hoffman (Act II)

Romeo and Juliet (Pas de deux)

Flower Festival at Genzano (Pas de deux)

Swan Lake (Act II)

Performances given in:
Perth	Sydney
Melbourne	Wellington
Adelaide	Dunedin

OCHTERTYRE THEATRE:
AUGUST 1974

Tales of Hoffmann (Pas de deux)

The Nutcracker (Act II pas de deux)

La Sylphide (Act II pas de deux)

Grand Pas Gitane
(16 August 1974)

AUTUMN TOUR:
OCTOBER-NOVEMBER 1974

Tales of Hoffmann

La Sylphide

La Ventana

Performances given in:
Hull	Glasgow
Nottingham	Liverpool
Stirling	Edinburgh

GALA PERFORMANCE: NOVEMBER 1974
(with Margot Fonteyn & Ivan Nagy)
King's Theatre, Glasgow

La Ventana

Intimate Pages

Music	Janácek
Choreography	Harold King
Design	Harold King

Valse Excentrique

Swan Lake (Act II Pas de deux)

The Dancing Floor
(2 November 1974, King's Theatre, Glasgow)

Music	Morton Subotnick
	(The Wild Bull)
Choreography	Jack Carter
Design	Norman McDowell

Love Duet from Romeo and Juliet

CHRISTMAS SEASON 1974
His Majesty's Theatre, Aberdeen

The Nutcracker

BALLET FOR SCOTLAND TOUR
FEBRUARY 1975

Scarlatti and Friends

Triptych

O Caritas

Nutcracker (Pas de deux)

Street Games

Performances given in:

Duns	Brora
Cumbernauld	Invergordon
Troon	Elgin
Dumbarton	Keith
Paisley	Kingussie
Greenock	Dumfries

SCOTTISH THEATRES TOUR: 1975

Intimate Pages

Flower Festival at Genzano (Pas de deux)

Three Dances to Japanese Music

Offenbach Variations

Performances given in:

Dundee	Kirkcaldy

SPRING TOUR: APRIL-MAY 1975

Giselle

La Fête Etrange

The Dancing Floor

Three Dances to Japanese Music

Paquita
(3 April 1975)

Music	Leon Minkus
Choreography	Joseph Mazilier
	& Marius Petipa
	(reproduced by Roland Casenave)
Design	Norman McDowell

Flower Festival at Genzano (Pas de deux)

Performances given in:

Edinburgh	Hull
Liverpool	Glasgow
Bath	Perth
Newcastle	Aberdeen

GALA PERFORMANCE
King's Theatre, Glasgow 12 May 1975
(with Maina Gielgud)

La Fête Etrange

Taras Bulba

Music	Vasily Solovyov-Syedoy
Choreography	Boris Feuster

O Caritas (premiere)

Forme et Ligne

Music	Pierre Henry
Choreography	Maurice Béjart

Spring Waters

Music	Rachmaninov
Choreography	Asaf Messerer
Staged by	Anna-Marie Holmes

Pas de Quatre

Music	Cesare Pugni
Choreography	Anton Dolin
Design	after the lithograph by Chalon

Paquita

SUMMER SEASON: AUGUST 1975
King's Theatre, Edinburgh

Giselle

The Nutcracker

La Sylphide

The Dancing Floor

INTERNATIONAL FESTIVAL OF DANCE
Madrid, 16-21 September, 1975

La Sylphide

Sonata à Trois

Paquita

Variations for Four
Music — Marguerite Keogh
Choreography — Anton Dolin

Flower Festival at Genzano (Pas de deux)

Three Dances to Japanese Music

Moment
Music — Ravel
Choreography — Murray Louis
Costumes — Barrow

The Lesson

INTERNATIONAL FESTIVAL OF BALLET
Barcelona, September 1975

Tales of Hoffmann

La Sylphide

Three Dances to Japanese Music

AUTUMN TOUR:
OCTOBER-NOVEMBER 1975

Intimate Pages

Harlequinade
Music — Riccardo Drigo
Choreography — Marius Petipa
(reproduced by John Gilpin)
Design — Gordon Garforth

O Caritas
Music & Lyrics — Andrea Toumazi,
Jeremy Taylor, Cat Stevens
Choreography — Peter Darrell

Le Corsaire (pas de deux)
Music — Riccardo Drigo
Choreography — Marius Petipa

The Scarlet Pastorale
(21 October 1975, King's Theatre, Edinburgh)
Music — Frank Martin
Choreography — Peter Darrell
Scenario — Peter Darrell
Design — Philip Prowse

Le Carnaval

Grande Pas Gitane

Pas de Quatre

Variations for Four

The Lesson

Performances given in:
Edinburgh — Aberdeen
Glasgow — Norwich

BALLET FOR SCOTLAND TOUR:
AUTUMN 1975

Beauty and the Beast

Flower Festival at Genzano

La Ventana

Pas de Quatre

Sonata à Trois

Performances given in:

Dunfermline	Dumfries
Largs	Montrose
Dunoon	Arbroath
Kilmarnock	Nairn
Prestwick	Dumbarton
Oban	Musselburgh

CHRISTMAS SEASON:
DECEMBER-JANUARY 1975-76
Theatre Royal, Glasgow

The Nutcracker

SPRING SEASON: MARCH 1976
Theatre Royal, Glasgow

Mary, Queen of Scots
(Premiered by The Scottish Ballet 3 March)
Music — John McCabe
Choreography — Peter Darrell
Scenario — Noël Goodwin
Design — Peter Docherty
Lighting — John B. Read

Tales of Hoffmann

Giselle

La Ventana

La Sylphide

Paquita

La Fête Etrange

"Paquita" with Andrea Durant
(Anthony Crickmay)   118

Pas de Quatre

Three Dances to Japanese Music

Le Carnaval

O Caritas

Jeux

The Lesson

SADLER'S WELLS SEASON: MARCH-APRIL 1976
Royal Gala Performance, 24 March
(with Margot Fonteyn and Anthony Dowell)

Paquita

Belong (London Première)

La Fête Etrange

The Scarlet Pastorale

Tales of Hoffmann

Mary, Queen of Scots

Giselle

Pas de Quatre

Three Dances to Japanese Music

Le Carnaval

O Caritas

Jeux

The Lesson

La Ventana

La Sylphide

SPRING TOUR: APRIL-MAY 1976

Mary, Queen of Scots

Tales of Hoffmann

La Ventana

Three Dances to Japanese Music

Nutcracker (Act II)

O Caritas

Pas de Quatre

Giselle

Performances given in:

Hull	Stirling
Edinburgh	Kirkcaldy
Liverpool	Perth
Inverness	Aberdeen

LONDON COLISEUM: JULY 1976
Nureyev Festival

La Sylphide

Three Dances to Japanese Music

Moment (London Premiere)

La Sylphide

The Lesson

SUMMER SEASON: AUGUST-SEPTEMBER 1976

Tales of Hoffmann

Giselle

Mary, Queen of Scots

Paquita

Othello

Belong

The Scarlet Pastorale

Performances given in:

Edinburgh	Aberdeen
Glasgow	

BALLET FOR SCOTLAND TOUR: NOVEMBER 1976

Soirée Musicale

Belong

O Caritas

Harlequinade

Othello

Performances given in:

Kilmarnock	Cumbernauld
Penicuik	Helensburgh
Dalkeith	Largs
Dumfries	Prestwick
Oban	Leven
Campbeltown	Falkirk
Hawick	Musselburgh
Dumbarton	Thurso
Dunoon	Brora
Paisley	Nairn
Ashington	Aboyne
Arbroath	

Andrea Durant and Paul Russell in "Ursprung"
(William Cooper) 120

CHRISTMAS SEASON: DECEMBER-JANUARY 1976-77
Lyceum Theatre, Edinburgh &
Theatre Royal, Glasgow

The Nutcracker

NUREYEV FESTIVAL FEBRUARY 1977
Palais des Sports, Paris
(with Nureyev and Makarova)

La Sylphide

Three Dances to Japanese Music

Giselle

SPRING TOUR: MARCH-MAY 1977

Swan Lake
(23 March 1977, King's Theatre, Edinburgh)

Music	Tchaikovsky
Choreography	Marius Petipa, Lev Ivanov, Peter Darrell
Production	Peter Darrell
Design	Peter Cazalet
Lighting	John B. Read

La Sylphide

Three Dances to Japanese Music

Performances given in:

Edinburgh	Wolverhampton
Aberdeen	Southsea
Inverness	Glasgow
Hull	

SUMMER SEASON: JULY-AUGUST 1977
Joint Season with Scottish Opera at King's Theatre, Edinburgh

The Nutcracker

Giselle

EDINBURGH FESTIVAL: AUGUST 1977
(with Bujones and Makarova)

1st Programmme

Les Sylphides

Othello

Don Quixote (Pas de deux)

The Scarlet Pastorale

2nd programme

La Sylphide

Three Dances to Japanese Music

SAN SEBASTIAN, BIARRITZ & ST. JEAN DE LUZ: SEPTEMBER 1977
(with Natalia Bessmertnova and Mikhail Lavrovsky)

1st programme

La Ventana

Spartacus (Pas de deux)

Cage of God

Don Quixote (Pas de deux)

Three Dances to Japanese Music

2nd programme

Les Sylphides

Spring Water (Pas de deux)

O Caritas

Swan Lake (Pas de deux)

Othello

BALLET FOR SCOTLAND TOUR: OCTOBER-NOVEMBER 1977

Suite from Les Sylphides

Don Quixote (Pas de deux)/
Flower Festival at Genzano (Pas de deux)

Cage of God

Swan Lake (Pas de deux)

Vespri

Performances given in

Falkirk	Dumbarton
Cumbernauld	Erskine
Musselburgh	Troon
Dundee	Dunoon
Aboyne	Kelso
Nairn	Hawick
Brora	Ashington
Fort William	St. Andrews
Oban	Penicuik
Campbeltown	Dalkeith
Kirkcaldy	Largs
Newcastle	Rothesay
Dumfries	

CHRISTMAS SEASON: DECEMBER-JANUARY 1977-78

The Nutcracker

Performances given in:
Aberdeen   Glasgow
Inverness

NEWORK '78: JANUARY 1978
Couper Institute, Glasgow

One Minus Two
Music   Schumann
Choreography   Roy Campbell-Moore

"Everybody's a Star"
Music   Hollywood Film Music, Led Zeppelin,
     Kinks, Genesis, Pink Floyd, John Lennon
Choreography   Peter Royston

Changing Music
Music   Focus, Debussy, Shostakovitch
Choreography   Peter Royston

Autumn
Music   Glazounov
Choreography   Gordon Aitken

In a White Room with Black Curtains
Music   Cream
Choreography   Anna McCartney

Memories of Nina
Music   Shostakovitch
Choreography   Roy Campbell-Moore

Three Songs
Music   Mahler
Choreography   William Bowen

Night on the Steppes
Music   Kabalevsky
Choreography   Christopher Blagdon,
                                        Serge Julien

Conflict
Music   Jesse Ehrlich
Choreography   Judy Mohekey

Lightforce
Music   Judith Earley
Choreography   Susan Cooper

Flower Walk
Music   Scott Joplin
Choreography   Christopher Long

6 Easy Pieces
Music   Jean-Michel Jarre
Choreography   Linden Currey

SPRING TOUR: APRIL-MAY 1978

Swan Lake

Les Sylphides

Jeux/Belong

Othello

Vespri

Performances given in:
Glasgow   Cardiff
Stirling   Hull
Edinburgh   Sunderland
Inverness   Darlington
Aberdeen   Perth

SUMMER SEASON: AUGUST 1978
King's Theatre, Edinburgh & Theatre Royal, Glasgow.

Napoli
(2nd August 1978, King's Theatre, Edinburgh)
Music   Gade, Helsted, Paulli and Lumbye
Choreography   August Bournonville
                          (reproduced by Poul Gnatt)
Design   Peter Cazalet
Lighting   John B. Read

Swan Lake Act II

Dancing Floor

Vespri

Tales of Hoffman

SANTANDER: AUGUST 1978
(with Galina Samsova)

1st programme

Swan Lake (Act II)

Dancing Floor

Walpurgis Night

Vespri

2nd programme

Les Sylphides

Othello

Sleeping Beauty

Three Dances to Japanese Music

123   Her Majesty Queen Elizabeth the Queen Mother
talks backstage at the Theatre Royal to David
Ashmole and Robin Duff, chairman of The
Scottish Ballet, after The Royal Gala performance
of "The Tales of Hoffmann"   (Gus Christie)

BALLET FOR SCOTLAND TOUR: SEPTEMBER-OCTOBER 1978

Naila
Music   Delibes
Choreography   Gordon Aitken
Design   Bruno Santini

Five Rückert Songs
Music   Mahler
Choreography   Peter Darrell

Beauty and the Beast

Napoli Variations

Performances given in:
Falkirk   Dumbarton
Penicuik   Dumfries
Musselburgh   Galashiels
Livingstone   Kelso
Troon   Hawick
Largs   Kirkcaldy
Rothesay   Dundee
Dunoon   Stirling
St. Andrews   Campbeltown
Montrose   Oban
Elgin   Aboyne
Fort William   Wick
Nairn   Thurso
Brora

OPEN HOUSE: 5-25 OCTOBER 1978
Works choreographed by members of the
company

CHRISTMAS SEASON: DECEMBER 1978
Theatre Royal, Glasgow

Swan Lake

The Nutcracker

NEWORK '79: JANUARY 1979
Eastwood Theatre, Glasgow

Aria
Music   Stravinsky (Violin Concerto in D)
Choreography   Garry Trinder

Herzgewächse
Music   Schoenberg (Herzgewachse op. 20)
Choreography   Erica Knighton

Snowflakes are Dancing
Music   Debussy (Clair de Lune)
Choreography   Michael Harper

Pastimes Passing
Music   Janácek (Sinfonietta)
Choreography   Ann Sholem

Love Story 2002
Music   Milhaud (La Création du Monde)
Choreogrpahy   Peter Royston

Dichotomy Singular
Music   Karel Husa (String Quartet No. 3)
Choreography   Roy Campbell-Moore

Rendezvous
Music   Debussy (1st Arabesque)
Choreography   Susan Cooper

Pteradacta
Music   Steve Miller Band
                               (Song for our Ancestors)
Choreography   Linden Currey

Symphony in C
Music   Stravinsky
Choreography   William Bowen

10th ANNIVERSARY SPRING TOUR: MARCH-JUNE 1979

Underground Rumours

Ursprung (The Source)
Music   Jon Anderson (of Yes)
Arranged by   Terry Davies
Choreography   Royston Maldoom
Design   Graham Bowers
Lighting   David Hersey

The Water's Edge
Music   Ian Anderson, David Palmer
               and Martin Barre (of Jethro Tull)
Choreography   Robert North
Design   Peter Farmer
Lighting   David Hersey

Such Sweet Thunder
Music   Duke Ellington (arranged by Paul Hart)
Choreography   Busby Berkeley
               (assisted by Peter Darrell)
Gowns by   Adrian (assisted by Bob Ringwood)
Lighting   Stanley McCandless
                               (recreated by David Hersey)

Napoli

Giselle

Tales of Hoffmann

Performances given in:
Glasgow   Hull
Edinburgh   Aberdeen
Coventry   Inverness
Hull   Darlington
Liverpool   Perth
Bournemouth

INDEX